The Ocean Plague

THE OCEAN PLAGUE.

THE OCEAN PLAGUE:

OR,

A VOYAGE TO QUEBEC IN AN IRISH EMIGRANT VESSEL.

EMBRACING

A QUARANTINE AT GROSSE ISLE IN 1847. WITH NOTES ILLUSTRATIVE OF
THE SHIP-PESTILENCE OF THAT FATAL YEAR.

BY A CABIN PASSENGER.

" To throw starving and diseased paupers under the rock at Quebec, ought to be punishable as murder."
LORD SYDENHAM.

BOSTON:
COOLIDGE AND WILEY, 12 WATER STREET.
1848.

CONTENTS.

CHAPTER IV.

An unwelcome follower. — A cheerless Sabbath. — A tempting cask. — Spread of fever. — Death and burial. — Sudden attacks. — Awful position. — Tough yarns. — A horrid spectacle. — A convalescent.

CHAPTER V.

Fog. — A scene of horror. — Speaking. — Sounding. — Death of two brothers. — Their burial. — Silent grief. — Phosphorescence. — Cod fishery. — The banks of Newfoundland. — Sickness among the crew. — Newfoundland coast. — Effect of fear. — An inheritance. — An auction.

CHAPTER VI.

Bearings. — Capes North and Ray. — Isle St. Paul. — Entrance of the gulf. — Jacques Cartier. — The Bird and Magdalen Islands. — Mackerel breeze. — Great take. — Anticosti. — Gaspé. — The river. — Aurora borealis. — A birth. — North shore. — A gale.

CHAPTER VII.

Calm after storm. — More deaths. — A take-in. — Charming vistas. — A delirious patient. — Kempt road. — Trois Pistolles. — A friendless burial. — Scarcity of water. — Mirage.

CHAPTER VIII.

A friendly sail. — Beautiful sunset. — A trial of patience. —

INTRODUCTION.

Men judge by the complexion of the sky,
The state and inclination of the day:
So may you by my dull and heavy eye,
My tongue hath but a heavier tale to say.
I play the torturer by small and small
To lengthen out the worst that may be spoken.
                                SHAKSPEARE.

EMIGRATION has for a long time been considered by
British political economists the most effective means of al-
leviating the grievous ills under which the Irish peasantry
labor. It is not our province to inquire into its expedi-
ency; but viewing the subject with the single eye of common-sense, it is difficult to see the necessity of expatriating
the superfluous population of a country wherein hundreds
of thousands of acres of land susceptible of the highest
culture, lie waste, — whose mines teeming with wealth
remain unworked, — and which is bordered by more than
two thousand miles of sea coast, whose banks swarm with
ling, cod, mackerel, &c., while salt-fish is largely imported
from Scotland.

Many years previous to legislators taking up the matter,
emigration from Ireland existed, and that of a class of
persons which could be badly spared from the already
impoverished island; consisting as it did of small but
substantial farmers, who perceiving but a gloomy prospect
before them, sold off their land, and, turning their capital
into cash, availed themselves of the opportunities that

2

existed to find comfort and independence by settling in America.

The majority of these adventurers being successful in their undertakings, they induced their relatives and friends to follow them ; and thus a strong tide of emigrants, whose number gradually increased each season, set toward the West.

This progressive and natural system of emigration, however, gave place within the last few years to a violent rush of famished, reckless human beings, flying from their native land, to seek food in a distant and unknown country.

The cause of this sudden change is easily ascertained. Every one is familiar with the wretched lot of the Irish peasantry, — obliged to work for a miserable pittance, their chief reliance was upon the crop of potatoes grown by each family in the little patch of ground attached to their hut; a poor dependence indeed, not only as regards the inferiority of the potato as the sole diet of a people, but from the great uncertainty always attending its propagation. The consequences of even a partial failure — an event of common occurrence — being of the most serious nature.

In the year 1822, the deficiency was so general that the price quadrupled, and the peasantry of the south and west were reduced to actual starvation. To alleviate the distress a committee was formed in London, and sub-committees throughout England; and such was the benevolence of individuals, that large funds were in a short time at their disposal. By the end of the year subscriptions had been raised in Great Britain amounting to £350,000; to which parliament added a grant of £300,000; while the local collections in Ireland were £150,000; making altogether

£800,000,— a large sum, but how inadequate to meet the wants of some three or four millions of starving people?

This serious warning it should be supposed would have opened the eyes of the country to the necessity of having something else as a resource under a similar emergency; but a plentiful season lulled them into forgetfulness of what they had suffered, and apathy concerning the future.

· So abundant was the produce of the seasons 1842 and 1843, that the poorest beggar refused potatoes, and they were commonly used to manure the land.

But the blight of the crop of 1845, and the total destruction of that of 1846, brought the country to the lowest ebb, and famine with its attendant, disease, stalked through the land.

Charity stretched forth her hand from far and near. America giving liberally of her abundance. But all that could be done fell far short of the wants of the dying sufferers. The government stepped forward, and advanced funds for the establishment of public works; this was attended with much advantage and mitigated a great deal of distress; but unfortunately, all the money had to be returned in the shape of onerous taxation upon the landowners.

The gentry became seriously alarmed, and some of them perceiving that the evil was likely to increase year after year, took into their consideration what would be the surest method of terminating it.

At length it was discovered that the best plan would be to get completely rid of those who were so heavy a burthen upon them, by shipping them to America; at the same time publishing to the world, as an act of brotherly love and kindness, a deed of crafty, calculating selfishness,—

for the expense of transporting each individual was less than the cost of one year's support in a workhouse.

It required but little argument to induce the prostrated people to accede to their landlords' proposal, by quitting their poverty-stricken country for " a land flowing with milk and honey," — poor creatures, they thought that any change would be for the better. They had nothing to risk, every thing to gain. " Ah! Sir," said a fellow-passenger to me, after bewailing the folly that tempted him to plunge his family into aggravated misfortune, — " we thought we could'nt be worse off than we war; but now to our sorrow we know the differ; for sure supposin we were dyin of starvation, or if the sickness overtuk us. We had a chance of a doctor, and if he could do no good for our bodies, sure the priest could for our souls; and then we'd be buried along wid our own people, in the ould church-yard, with the green sod over us; instead of dying like rotten sheep thrown into a pit, and the minit the breath is out of our bodies, flung into the sea to be eaten up by them horrid sharks."

It cannot excite the least surprise that these wretched beings should carry with them the seeds of that plague from which they were flying; and it was but natural that these seeds should rapidly germinate in the hot-bed holds of ships crammed almost to suffocation with their distempered bodies. In short, nothing was wanted to encourage the speedy development of the direst disease and misery; but alas! every thing that could check their spread was absent.

My heart sickens when I think upon the fatal scenes of the awfully tragic drama enacted upon the wide stage of the

Atlantic ocean, in the floating lazar houses that were wafted upon its bosom during the never-to-be-forgotten year 1847.

Without a precedent in history, may God grant that the account of it may descend to posterity without a parallel.

Laws for the regulation of passenger ships were in existence; but whether on account of difficulty arising from the vast augmentation of number, or some other cause, they (if at all put in force) proved quite ineffectual.

What a different picture was presented by the Germans who migrated in large bodies? who,—although the transmission of human beings from Fatherland must always be attended by more or less pain and trouble,—underwent none of those heart-rending trials reserved exclusively for the Irish emigrant.

Never did so many souls tempt all the dangers of the deep, to seek asylums in an adopted country; and, could we draw a veil over the sad story of the ship pestilence, " this migration of masses, numbering of late years more than 100,000 annually, now to nearly 300,000 annually, not in the warlike spirit of the Goths and Vandals who overran the Roman Empire, and destroyed the monuments of art and evidences of civilization, but in the spirit of peace, anxious to provide for themselves and their children the necessaries of life, and apparently ordained by Providence to relieve the countries of the old world, and to serve great purposes of good to mankind,— is one of the most interesting spectacles the world ever saw."[*]

The reader must not expect to find any thing more in these pages than a faithful detail of the occurrences on board an emigrant vessel. The author has no desire to

* Immigration into the United States. By J. Chickering. Boston, 1848.

exaggerate, were it possible to do so. And he who wishes to arrive at any conclusion as to the amount of suffering, must calculate, from the affliction that I have faintly portrayed upon a small scale, what must have been the unutterable " weight of woe " in ships whose holds contained five or six hundred tainted, famished, dying mortals.

The following extract from the London Times newspaper presents a faithful and graphic review of the dire tragedy.

" The great Irish famine and pestilence will have a place in that melancholy series of similar calamities to which historians and poets have contributed so many harrowing details and touching expressions. Did Ireland possess a writer endued with the laborious truth of Thucydides, the graceful felicity of Virgil, or the happy invention of De Foe, the events of this miserable year might be quoted by the scholar for ages to come, together with the sufferings of the pent-up multitudes of Athens, the distempered plains of northern Italy, or the hideous ravages of our own great plague. But time is ever improving on the past. There is one horrible feature of the recent, not to say present visitation, which is entirely new. The fact of more than a hundred thousand souls flying from the very midst of a calamity across a great ocean to a new world, crowding into insufficient vessels, scrambling for a footing on a deck, or a berth in a hold, committing themselves to these worse than prisons, while their frames were wasted with ill fare and their blood infected with disease, fighting for months of unutterable wretchedness against the elements without and pestilence within, giving almost hourly victims to the deep, landing at length on shores already terrified and diseased, consigned to environments of the living and the dead, spreading death wherever they come, and having no other prospect before them than a long continuance of these horrors in a still farther flight across forests and lakes under a Canadian sun and a Canadian frost — all these are circumstances beyond the experience of the Greek historian or Latin poet, and such as an Irish gentleman alone could produce.

"By the end of the season there is little doubt that the emigration into Canada alone will have amounted to 100,000; nearly all from Ireland. We know the condition in which these poor creatures embarked on their perilous adventure. They were only living men and women. On the authority of the Montreal Board I am enabled to say that they were hurried … two or three times greater than … have presumed to carry on …

"The worse horrors of the massacre … boast or the ambition of his … cost, have been menaced … from their native homes … arrived at Montreal in … Liverpool out of 145 … passage, and 345 … were visibly diseased … number had in them … says the Board of Health … morning from … 108 died on the passage …

"The Virginus … sage. 158 … tottering; the captain …

" The Blackhole of Calcutta was a mercy compared to the holds of these vessels. Yet simultaneously, as if in reproof of those on whom the blame of all this wretchedness must fall, foreigners, Germans from Hamburg and Bremen are daily arriving, all healthy, robust, and cheerful.

" This vast unmanageable tide of population thus thrown upon Montreal, like the fugitives from some bloody defeat, or devastated country, has been greatly augmented by the prudent, and, we must add, most necessary precautions adopted in time by the United States, where most stringent sanitary regulations, enforced by severe penalties, have been adopted to save the ports of the Union from those very horrors which a paternal government has suffered to fall upon Montreal. Many of these pest ships have been obliged to alter their destination, even while at sea, for the St. Lawrence.

" At Montreal a large proportion of these outcasts have lingered from sheer inability to proceed. The inhabitants of course have been infected.

" A still more horrible sequel is to come. The survivors have to wander forth and find homes. Who can say how many will perish on the way, or the masses of houseless, famished, and half-naked wretches that will be strewed on the inhospitable snow when a Canadian winter sets in ?

" Of these awful occurrences some account must be given. Historians and politicians will some day sift and weigh the conflicting narrations and documents of this lamentable year, and pronounce with or without affectation, how much is due to the inclemency of heaven, and how much to the cruelty, heartlessness or improvidence of man. The boasted institutions and spirit of the empire are on trial. They are weighed in the balance.

" Famine and pestilence are at the gates, and the conscience-stricken nation will almost fear to see the 'writing on the wall.'

" We are forced to confess that, whether it be the fault of our laws or our men, this new act in the terrible drama has not been met as humanity and common-sense would enjoin. The result was quite within the scope of calculation, and even of care."

Miscalculation, and want of care, are terms far too mild to apply to such wanton negligence as resulted in the immediate sacrifice of upwards of 25,000 souls, four fifths of whom fell upon their way to Canada. From the report issued at the end of the season, it appears that, of the 98,105 (of whom 60,000 were Irish) that were shipped for Quebec,

There died at sea,	5,293
At Grosse Isle and Quebec,	8,072
In and above Montreal,	7,000
Making	20,365,

besides those who afterwards perished, whose number can never be ascertained. Allowing an average of·300 persons to each, 200 vessels were employed in the transmission to Canada of Irish emigrants alone ; and each of these vessels lost one third of her living cargo ere she again set sail upon her return to Europe.

If we suppose those 60,000 persons to be an army on their way to invade some hostile power, how serious would appear the loss of one third of their number before a battle was fought ? Yet the 40,000 who landed upon the Canadian shores had to fight many a deadly battle before

2*

they could find peace or rest. Or, in order to make the matter sensible to those who know the value of money better than of human life, let us multiply 20,000 by 5, the cost in pounds sterling of the passage of each individual, and we perceive a loss of £100,000, or $500,000 dollars.

But it may be thought that the immolation of so many wretched starvelings was rather a benefit than a loss to the world. *It may be so. Yet—untutored, degraded, famished, and plague-stricken, as they were; I assert that there was more true heroism, more faith, more forgiveness to their enemies, and submission to the Divine Will, exemplified in these victims, than could be found in ten times the number of their oppressors.

CHAPTER I.

Each moment plays
His little weapon in the narrower sphere
Of sweet domestic comfort, and cuts down
The fairest bloom of sublunary bliss.
Bliss — sublunary bliss ; — proud words and vain,
Implicit treason to divine decree,
A bold invasion of the rights of heaven,
I clasp'd the phantoms, and I found them air.
O, had I weighed it ere my fond embrace,
What darts of agony had miss'd my soul.

YOUNG.

May 30th, 1847.

MANY and deep are the wounds that the sensitive heart inflicts upon its possessor, as he journeys through life's pilgrimage ; but on few occasions are they so acutely felt, as when one is about tó part from those who formed a portion of his existence ; deeper still pierces the pang as the idea presents itself that the separation may be for ever ; but when one feels a father's nervous grasp, — a dear sister's tender, sobbing embrace ; and the eye wanders around the apartment drinking in each familiar object, until it rests upon the vacant chair which she who nursed his helpless infancy was wont to occupy, then the agony he wishes to conceal becomes insupportable. But as the skilful surgeon tears off the bandage which the hand of affection gently withdraws from the wound,— thereby unconsciously inflicting greater pain ; so it is better not to linger upon the affecting scene ; but rush suddenly away.

It was a charming morning on which I left dear old Ireland;—the balmy new-born day, in all the freshness of early summer, was gladdened by the beams of the sun which rose above the towers of the city, sunk in undisturbed repose. It was a morning calculated to inspire the drooping soul with hope; auguring future happiness.

Too soon I arrived at the quay, and left my last footprint on my native land. The boat pushed off, and in a few minutes I was on board the brig that was to waft me across the wide Atlantic.

There was not a soul on deck; but presently the grizzled head of the captain was protruded from the cabin; and from the uninviting aspect of his face I feared that he would prove an unsocial companion for a long voyage. He received me as kindly as his stubborn nature would allow; and I was forced to admire the manly dignity of the rude tar, when, from the bent attitude he was obliged to assume while ascending the companion ladder, he stood upright on the deck. The sailors now issued from the forecastle, and the mate came up and introduced himself to me.

The captain having given the word to weigh anchor, a bustle immediately arose throughout the vessel; the seamen promptly proceeded to their work, with apparent pleasure; although (being the Sabbath) they did not accompany the action with the usual chant. The chain having become entangled in the cables of some fishing boats, it was a considerable while before the anchor was hoisted. At length, the top-sails were unreefed, and our bark glided through the beauteous bay.

In a short time we rounded the promontory of Howth; having taken the north channel as the wind was southerly.

The captain then led me down to the cabin for breakfast, and introduced me to his wife, who, he informed
me, always accompanied him to sea, and whom I shall for
the future designate as the mistress, — as by that term she
was known to both crew and passengers. Feeling an inclination towards squeamishness, and being much more
sick at heart, I retired to my state-room! and lying down
upon the berth, fell into a dreamy slumber, in which I
remained until aroused; when I found it was late in the
afternoon, and tea was ready. I felt somewhat revived by
the grateful beverage; and accompanied the captain on
deck. We were off Carlingford, and the mountains of
Mourne. The passengers were cooking their evening
meal at their fires upon the fore-deck; and the sailors
discussing their coffee in the forecastle. I endeavored to
enter into conversation with the captain, but he was pro-
vokingly taciturn; however, we were soon joined by the
mistress, who was not unwilling to make up for her husband's deficiency. The sun set; and twilight subsided
into darkness; a cold night breeze also told that it was
time to go below.

Monday, May 31st.

I rose early, and inhaled the fresh morning air. We
made good progress during the night, and the bold cliffs of
the coast of Antrim were visible on one hand, the Scotch
shore on the other. At 8, A. M., the bell rang for breakfast, and I took my seat opposite the captain. The mistress sat in an arm-chair, and the mate on a stool next me,
completing the cabin circle. We were attended by Simon
the cabin-boy, whom at first sight I took to be a " darky."
His face was coated with smoke and soot, streaked by

the perspiration that trickled from his brow, which was
surmounted by a thicket of short, wiry black hair, standing
on end; his lustreless brown eyes I cannot better describe
than by borrowing a Yankee illustration : they were " like
two glass balls lighted by weak rush lights ; " — his lips
were thick, straight, and colorless; his complexion, (when
unveiled) was a grimy yellow ; — and the expression of
his wide flat face, idiotic. He wore a red flannel shirt,
and loose blue pilot trowsers ; but neither shoes, nor
stockings ; his movements were slow, except at meals,
when he seemed to regain his suspended animation ; and
it was a goodly sight to see him gulping coffee, bolting
dodges of fat pork, and crunching hard biscuit, as raven-
ously as a hungry bear.

No two specimens of human nature could possibly present more striking contrasts than Simon and his fellow-
apprentice Jack. The latter was about 15 years of age,
remarkably small and active. Squirrel never climbed tree
more nimbly than Jack could go aloft ; and in the accom-
plishments of chewing and smoking he might compete
with the oldest man aboard ; his fair skin was set off by
rosy cheeks ; and his sparkling blue eyes beamed with —
devilment. He was a favorite of every one except the
mistress, with whom his pranks did not pass, being therefore exempt from the menial offices of cabin boy, which
devolved upon Simon ; his principal amusement consisted
in persecuting that genius.

The mate was a very little man, not more than five feet
high ; but in excellent condition, as seamen generally are ;
he was lame in one leg ; which deformity he took great
pains to hide ; causing a constrained limp that was ex-

tremely ludicrous; he was well-looking, and sported a
capacious pair of black whiskers, the outline of which he
frequently altered. He had been a " captain," but unfortunately, loving the bottle, he lost his "caste." ,There existed
little confidence between him and the captain ; and both
being of a warm temperament, there were occasional
symptoms of collision; but they were prevented from
ending in open rupture by the timely interference of the
mistress, on whom the captain would let loose his wrath,
which though expressed in no gentle terms, she bore with
exemplary patience.

The mistress was small, ruddy, and sun-burnt; having
seen some sixty winters, forty of which she had spent at
sea,—generally in the home trade; but varied occasionally
by a voyage to Russia, or to America. She was in the
habit of keeping a private log, in which she noted the
incidents of her travels. I was allowed to look into this
interesting production, which amused me no less by the
originality of the orthography, than its elegance of diction.
Being a native of Cumberland, her pronunciation was
not particularly euphonious; she also, when addressing her
husband, the mate, and all familiar acquaintances, used
the terms " thee " and " thou," invariably reversing their
grammatical order.   •

Tuesday, June 1st.

. After breakfast, the mate invited me to see the depot of
provisions. I accordingly followed him, descending by a
ladder into an apartment partitioned off from the hold, and
dividing it from the cabin.

By the light from the lantern I perceived a number of
sacks, which were filled with oatmeal and biscuit. The

mate having proceeded to prepare the passengers' rations for distribution, I sat down upon one of the sacks, from beneath which suddenly issued a groan. I jumped up, quite at a loss to account for the strange sound, and looked at the mate, in order to discover what he thought of it. He seemed somewhat surprised; but in a moment removed two or three sacks; and lo! there was a man crouched up in a corner. As he had not seen him before, the mate at once concluded that he was a "stowaway," so giving him a shake to make him stand upright, he ordered him to mount the ladder, bestowing a kick upon the poor wretch to accelerate his tardy ascent.

The captain was summoned from below, and a council immediately held for the trial of the prisoner, who confessed, that not having enough of money to pay for his passage, he bribed the watchman employed to prevent the possibility of such an occurrence. He had been concealed for three days, but at night made his way into the hold, through a breach in the partition: his presence was therefore known to some of the passengers. He had no clothes but the rags he wore; nor had he any provisions. To decide what was to be done with him was now the consideration, but the captain hastily terminated the deliberation, by swearing that he should be thrown overboard. The wretched creature was quite discomfited by the captain's wrath, and earnestly begged for forgiveness. It was eventually settled that he should be landed upon the first island at which we should touch; with which decision he appeared to be quite satisfied. He said that he was willing to work for his support; but the captain swore determinedly that he should not taste one pound of the ship's provision. He was therefore left to the tender mercies of his fellow-passengers.

In consequence of this discovery, there was a general muster in the afternoon, affording me an opportunity of seeing all the emigrants; and a more motley crowd I never beheld; — of all ages, from the infant to the feeble grandsire and withered crone.

While they were on deck, the hold was searched, but without any further discovery, no one having been found below but a boy, who was unable to leave his berth, from debility. Many of them appeared to me to be quite unfit to undergo the hardship of a long voyage; but they were inspected and passed by a doctor, although the captain, as he informed me, protested against taking some of them. One old man was so infirm, that he seemed to me to be in the last stage of consumption.

The next matter to be accomplished was to regulate the allowance of provisions to which each family was entitled. One pound of meal or of bread being allowed for each adult, — half a pound for each individual under fourteen years of age, — and one third of a pound for each child under seven years. Thus, although there were 110 souls, great and small, they counted as 84 adults. That was, therefore, the number of pounds to be issued daily. On coming on board, provisions for a week were distributed; but as they wasted them most improvidently, they had to be served again to-day. The mate consequently determined to give out the day's rations every morning.

Wednesday, June 2nd.

We made but little progress during the night, and were

still in the channel, within sight of the Mull of Cantire, and the northern shore of Ireland.

Having but a few books with me, I seized upon a greasy old volume of sundry magazines, which I found in the cabin. I also commenced the study of a book of navigation. These, varied with the Book of books, Shakspeare, and Maunder's Treasuries, kept me free from ennui. When tired of reading, I had ample scope for observation.

The mistress spent the forenoon fishing, and the afternoon in curing the mackerel and gurnet she caught. We had some at tea, when I met with a deprivation I had not anticipated;—there was no milk! and I did not at all relish my tea without it. One cup was quite enough for me; but I soon became habituated to it. Having rounded the long promontory of Donegal, the outline of the shore became indistinct; and making our calculations not to see land again for some time, the mate took his "departure" from Malin Head.

CHAPTER II.

Roll on, thou dark and deep blue ocean, roll !

BYRON.

June 3d.

WHEN I came on deck this morning, I found that we were sailing upon the bosom of the broad Atlantic, no object being visible to relieve the vast expanse of water and sky, except the glorious sun ; and as I turned my eyes from the survey of the distant horizon, and fixed them upon the little bark that wafted us, a sensation akin to that of the " Ancient Mariner " possessed my mind.

> " Alone, alone, all, all alone,
> Alone on a wide, wide sea."

As the boy who was unable to attend the muster still continued ill, and was reported to be feverish, the mistress and I reviewed the medicine chest. We found it to contain a jar of castor oil, epsom salts, laudanum, hartshorn, &c.; also a book of directions, which were by no means explicit, and they so perplexed the mistress, even with the aid of her spectacles, that as she was nothing the wiser of the study, she resolved to trust to her own experience in the concoction of a dose. The mate took his first observation at noon ; and as he stood peering through the eye-hole of the quadrant, he reminded me forcibly of poor old uncle Sol's little midshipman.

The passengers' fire-places, upon either side of the
fore-deck, furnished endless scenes, sometimes of noisy
merriment, at others of quarrels. The fire was contained
in a large wooden case, lined with bricks and shaped
something like an old-fashioned settee; the coals being
confined by two or three iron bars in front. From morning till evening they were surrounded by groups of men,
women and children; some making " stirabout," in all
kinds of vessels, and others baking cakes upon extempo-
rary griddles. These cakes were generally about two
inches thick, and when baked were encased in a burnt
crust coated with smoke, being actually raw in the centre.
Such was the unvaried food of the greater number of these
poor creatures. A few of them, who seemed to be better
off, had herrings, or bacon. The meal with which they
were provided was of very bad quality; — this they had
five days; and biscuit, which was good, two days in the
week.

Friday, June 4th.

The sailors and apprentices were (as the mate expressed
it in his log) variously employed, — mending sails, tarring
ropes, spinning yarns, &c. Sailors sit and sew very differ-
ently from tailors; instead of doubling up their legs under
them, they stretch them out straight before them as they sit
upon the deck. Their thimble is also peculiar, not being
worn on the top of the finger, but upon the ball of the
thumb, to which it is fastened by a leather strap, buckled
round the wrist. I was surprised at the expedition and
neatness with which they sewed, with their coarse needles
and long threads.

Jack created some diversion by daubing a " gossoon's "

face with tar, and shaving him with a rusty knife. It was
exhilarating to hear the children's merry laughter;—poor
little things, they seemed quite reconciled with their situa-
tion! I learned that many of these emigrants had never
seen the sea nor a ship, until they were on board. They
were chiefly from the county Meath, and sent out at the
expense of their landlord, without any knowledge of the
country to which they were going, or means of livelihood,
except the labor of the father of each family. All they
knew concerning Canada was, that they were to land in
Quebec, and to go up the country; moreover, they had a
settled conviction that the voyage was to last exactly three
weeks. In addition to these there were a few who were
going to try their fortunes on their own account. One of
the latter was a Connaught "boy," who having lived upon
the coast and spent his time partly in fishing, made himself
useful about the brig, and thereby ingratiated himself into
favor with the captain, and the consequent jealousy of his
fellow-passengers, who, thinking him rather soft, took
pleasure in teasing him. Two young men from Kilkenny,
and one from the county Clare, completed the list. The
former used to astonish the Meath-men with the triple
wonders of their native city.

Saturday, June 5th.

As the passengers had a great inclination to infringe
upon the after-deck, the captain drew a line, the penalty
for crossing which was the stoppage of a day's water.

I observed the sea to be crowded with myriads of slimy
looking objects, which the sailors called "slobbs." They
varied in size, form, and color; some of them resembling
a lemon cut in half. How beautiful also was the lumi-

nous appearance of the water at night, which I delighted to watch, as we glided through the liquid fire.

Nor was it less pleasing to observe the "Portuguese men of war," with their tiny sails set to the breeze, and surmounting the crests of the rolling billows. I had a rummage through the charts, and enjoyed a practical lecture upon them, with illustrative lectures by the mistress, enlivened, by way of episode, with occasional contradictions by the captain, who with rule and compass traced our progress daily upon the great chart of the North Atlantic ocean. We had two ships in company with us all the day; but they were too distant to distinguish their names. One of the passengers having thrown the Connaughtman's hat overboard, the captain gave him a blue and white striped night-cap, with which on his head he strutted about, much to the amusement of the youngsters, one of whom attached a rope to the tail of his coat; this he dragged after him for some time, until Jack changed the scene by cutting the tail off. When Paddy discovered his loss, he was outrageous, and made a grievous complaint to the mate, who doctored the coat by abstracting the other tail, thereby transforming the garment into a jacket. When the matter came to the captain's ears, he presented Paddy with an old pilot jacket, which made a great coat for him; he was therefore no loser by the affair.

· Sunday, June 6th.

The favorable breeze that carried us out of the channel having forsaken us, the little progress we made was gained by tacking, which kept the sailors constantly employed. The passengers were dressed in their best clothes; and presented a better appearance than I expected. The sailors also donned their holiday toggery in the afternoon.

A group of young men being at a loss for amusement, began to wrestle and play "pitch and toss;" but the mate soon put a stop to their diversions; at which they grumbled, saying that "they did'nt think that Mr. Mate would be so hard."

Very few of them could read; neither did they seem to have any regard for the sanctity of the Sabbath. In the evening they had prayers in the hold; and were divided into two parties, — those who spoke Irish, and those who did not; each section having a leader, who gabbled in his respective language a number of " Paters and Aves," as quickly as the devotees could count their beads.

After these religious exercises they came upon deck, and spent the remainder of the day jesting, laughing, and singing.

We had a clear and beautiful sunset; from which the captain prognosticated an easterly wind.

CHAPTER III.

Thou shalt not be afraid for any terror by night, nor for the arrow that flieth by day; for the pestilence that walketh in darkness, nor for the sickness that destroyeth in the noon-day. — PSALMS OF DAVID.

June 7th.

The passengers elected four men to govern their commonwealth, the principal of whom had the title of "Head committee." The other three being inactive, the sole authority was wielded by him, much to the terror of the little boys, who were often uproarious, and to keep whom in order he frequently administered the "cat."

The other duties of this functionary consisted in seeing that the hold was kept clean; in preventing smoking below, settling differences, &c. He was also the medium of communication with the "other house," he and Paddy alone being permitted to go aft.

Tuesday, June 8th.

We steered a southward course, but gained very little longitude.

The two ships were again in sight; one was the *Tamerlane* of Aberistwyth; the other the *Virginius* of Liverpool; both fine vessels, with passengers.

The head committee reported that two women were ill; they were therefore dosed according to the best skill of the mistress, who was desirous of going into the hold to see them; but the captain peremptorily desired her upon no account to do so; and kept a sharp lookout, that she might not visit them unknown to him.

The boy, whom nothing ailed but sea-sickness and fatigue, had recovered. I saw him upon deck, — a miserable looking little animal, with a huge misshapen head, sallow, lantern-jaws, and glassy eyes; — apparently about twelve years of age; but his father said that he was twenty. I could scarcely credit him, but was assured of the fact by his neighbours, who said that he always had the same emaciated appearance, although he never before complained of illness. He went by the name of " The little shoemaker."

Wednesday, June 9th.

As we were seated at dinner, in the cabin, discussing a savory dish of " Lobscouse ". made by the mistress, we were alarmed by the shouting of men, and screaming of women.

We hurried on deck, thinking that some one was overboard, and judge of our terror, when we saw the fore part of the brig in a blaze. All hands having assisted, a plentiful supply of water in a short time subdued the fire, which extended no further than the caboose; it arose from the negligence of Simon, who fell asleep, leaving a lighted candle stuck against the boards. This was the only brilliant act of which he was guilty during the voyage, and as a reward for which the mate bestowed upon him a rope's end.

Thursday, June 10th.

The only incidents of the day were, breakfast, dinner, and supper, — the meridional observation, and the temporary stir consequent on the captain coming upon deck after

3

a "snooze," and shouting out "'bout ship." Some more cases of illness were reported; and the mistress was kept busy mixing medicine, and making drinks; hoping that by early attention the sickness might be prevented from spreading.

Friday, June 11th.

As I was pacing the deck in the afternoon, I observed one of the passengers,—a well looking man, with fine brown eyes, timidly approach me. After looking about him, to assure himself that the captain was below, he doffed his hat and addressed me as follows: "I beg your honor's pardon, but I hope it's no offence." Having told him that he had given me none, he proceeded,—"Well then master, is'nt it mighty quare intirely, and how can the likes of us know the differ; but I hope your honor it's all right?" I replied that I was not aware of any thing being wrong, and desired him to say what was the danger he feared, which caused him to ask; "Aragh! why thin are we goin back to ould Ireland?" I demanded his reason for such a supposition; when after scratching his head, and casting a glance towards the cabin, looking rather perplexed, he went on, "That little gossoon of mine, your honor,—a mighty smart chap he is too, and a great scholiar entirely, he tould us,—but faith! I dunno how to believe him,—though he got his larnin at the national school, and can cast up figures equal to the agint, and can read the whole side of a book without stoppin,—he says sir,—that the sun, God bless it, sets in the wist." Here he paused and looked earnestly at me, as if for a confirmation of the fact. I therefore said that the boy's knowledge was pretty accurate. Seeming encouraged, he continued — "Moreover than that, he says that Ameriky, where we all are goin to, if the Almighty God spares us, (here he crossed himself) glory be to his name! it's in the wist of the world too." He again paused, and looked enquiringly. "Well," said I, "he is pretty right there also, America is west from Ireland." "Then master, here's what we want to come at, you see. If Ameriky is in the wist, musn't the sun set in it,—then why is it, your honor, that instead of followin it, we're runnin away from it as hard as we can lick?" Such was the fact,—a fresh northerly breeze compelling us to bear to the south-east. I now saw the nature of the problem he wished to have solved, and explained the matter as explicitly as I possibly could; but it was some time before he comprehended me. At length he seemed to become enlightened on the subject, for, giving his thigh a slap of his open palm, he exclaimed, "Och! by the powers, I see it all now; it's as plain as a pike-staff; and I'm sure I'm obleeged to your honor, and so is the gossoon too.—Oh, that divil's clip,— Jack; wait till I ketch him. If I don't murder him it's no matter. What do you think your honor, he tould the little chap, when he axed him all about it? 'Why,' says he, 'sure we're goin back again for the mistress' nittin needles, that she forgot.' So as he wouldn't tell him, nor none of the sailors, I made bould to ax your honor, as the little chap was loth to make so free."

On the conclusion of the dialogue, Jack,—who was over our heads, in the shrouds,—burst into a hearty fit of laughter. In which I could not but participate, when I noticed the comicality of the arch sailor-boy's appearance, and the simplicity of my interlocutor, who, hearing the

captain's heavy step coming up the ladder, hastily retired,
vowing vengeance upon Jack.

Saturday, June 12th.

I amused myself taking a sketch of the cabin "interior." It was about ten feet square, and so low that the
only part of it in which the captain could stand upright,
was under the skylight. At either side was a berth; both
of which were filled with the mistress' boxes, the captain's
old clothes, old sails, and sundry other articles, which were
there stowed away, and concealed from view by chintz
curtains, trimmed with white cotton fringe. The ceiling
was garnished with numerous charts rolled up, and confined by tapes running from beam to beam; from one of
which, — carefully covered by a cotton handkerchief, —
was suspended the captain's new hat. A small recess
above the table contained a couple of wine glasses, one of
them minus the shank; also an antique decanter, resting
upon an old quarto prayer-book, and guarded by a dangerous looking blunderbuss, which was supported by two
brass hooks, from one of which hung a small bag containing the captain's spectacles, rule, pencil, and compass. At
each side of this recess was a locker: one of them containing a crock of butter, and another of eggs, besides
tobacco and soap; the other held a fine Cheshire cheese,
a little keg of sprats, and other articles too numerous to
mention. An unhappy canary, perched within a rusty
cage, formed a pendant from the centre of the sky-light,
but a much more pleasing picture decorated one of the
panels, — a still-life, admirably delineating an enormous
flitch of bacon, which daily grew — less. A small door led
into the captain's state-room; the ceiling of which was

tastefully ornamented by several bunches of dipt candles;
while the narrow shelves groaned under the weight of,—
jars of sugar, preserves, bottled porter, spices and the other
usual necessaries for a long voyage. I was disturbed in
the progress of my portraiture by the mistress, who came
down to warm a drink at the stove, for some of the sick
folks. The two women who first became ill, were said to
show symptoms of bad fever; and additional cases of
illness were reported by the Head committee. The
patients begged for an increased allowance of water;
which could not be granted, as the supply was very
scanty; two casks having leaked.

Sunday, June 13th.

The reports from the hold became very alarming; and
the mistress was occupied all day attending the numerous
calls upon her. She already regretted having come the
voyage; but her kind heart did not allow her to consult
her ease. When she appeared upon deck, she was beset
by a crowd of poor creatures, each having some request to
make; often of a most inconsiderate kind, and few of
which it was in her power to comply with. The day was
cold and cheerless; and I occupied myself reading in the
cabin.

Monday, June 14th.

The Head committee brought a can of water to show
it to the captain: it was quite foul, muddy, and bitter from
having been in a wine cask. When allowed to settle it
became clear, leaving considerable sediment in the bottom
of the vessel; but it retained its bad taste. The mate
endeavoured to improve it by trying the effect of charcoal,
and of alum; but some of the casks were beyond remedy,

and the contents, when pumped out, resembled nauseous
ditch water. There were now eight cases of serious illness; — six of them being fever and two dysentery; —
the former appeared to be of a peculiar character, and very
alarming: the latter disease did not seem to be so violent
in degree.

Tuesday, June 15th.

The reports this morning were very afflicting, and I felt
much, that I was unable to render any assistance to my
poor fellow-passengers. The captain desired the mistress
to give them every thing out of his own stores that she
considered would be of service to any of them. He felt
much alarmed; nor was it to be wondered at that con-
tagious fever, — which under the most advantageous circumstances, and under the watchful eyes of the most skilful physicians, baffles the highest ability, — should terrify
one having the charge of so many human beings, likely to
fall a prey to the unchecked progress of the dreadful disease; for once having shown itself in the unventilated hold
of a small brig, containing one hundred and ten living
creatures, how could it possibly be stayed, — without suit-
able medicines, medical skill, or even pure water to slake
the patient's burning thirst?

The prospect before us was indeed an awful one; and
there was no hope for us but in the mecry of God.

Wednesday, June 16th.

The past night was very rough, and I enjoyed little rest.
No additional cases of sickness were reported: but there
were apparent signs of insubordination amongst the healthy
men, who complained of starvation, and the want of water

to make drinks for their sick wives and children. A deputation came aft to acquaint the captain with their griev-
ances, but he ordered them away, and would not listen
to a word from them. When he went below, the ring-
leader threatened that they would break into the provision
store.

The mate did not take any notice of the threat, but repeated to me, in their hearing, an anecdote of his own
experience when a captain; showing with what determi-
nation he suppressed an outbreak in his vessel. He concluded by alluding to cutlasses, and the firearms in the
cabin. And in order to make a deeper impression on
their minds, he brought up the old blunderbuss, from which
he fired a shot, the report of which was equal to that of a
small cannon. The deputation slunk away, muttering
complaints.

If they were resolute, they might easily have seized upon the provisions. In fact, I was surprised how famished
men could so patiently bear with their own, and their
starved children's sufferings; but the captain would wil-
lingly have listened to them if it were in his power to relieve their distress.

Thursday, June 17th.

Two new cases of fever were announced, and from
the representation of the mate, — the poor creatures in the
hold were in a shocking state. The men who suffered
from dysentery were better; the mistress's prescription —
flour porridge with a few drops of laudanum — having
given them relief. The requests of the friends of the fever
patients were most preposterous; — some asking for beef,
others wine. They were all desirous of laudanum being

administered to them in order to procure sleep; but we were afraid to dispense so dangerous a remedy, except with extreme caution. Our progress was almost imperceptible, and the captain began to grow very uneasy, there being at the rate of the already miserable allowance of food, but provisions for fifty days. It also now became necessary to reduce the complement of water, and to urge the necessity of using sea water in cookery.

Friday, June 18th.

The fire-places were the scenes of endless contentions. The sufferings they endured appeared to embitter the wretched emigrants one against another. Their quarrels were only ended when the fires were extinguished, at 7 o'clock, p. m.; at which time they were surrounded by squabbling groups, preparing their miserable evening meal. They would not leave until Jack mounted the shrouds of the fore-mast, and precipitated a bucket full of water on each fire; when they snatched up their pots and pans, and, half blinded by the steam, descended into the hold, with their half cooked suppers. Although Jack delighted in teasing them, they never complained of his pranks, however annoying.

CHAPTER IV.

I saw the seven angels which stood before God; and to them were given
seven trumpets. . . . . .
And the seven angels which had the seven trumpets prepared themselves to
sound. . . . . .
And the seventh angel sounded. . . . . . .
And the sea gave up the dead which were in it; and death and hell delivered
up the dead which were in them: and they were judged every man. . . .
REVELATIONS.

June 19th.

A shark followed us all the day, and the mate said it
was a certain forerunner of death. The cabin was like an
apothecary's shop, and the mistress a perfect slave. I endeavoured to render her every assistance in my power.
The mate also was indefatigable in his exertions to alleviate
the miserable lot of our helpless human cargo. Not
having seen the "stowaway" on deck for some time, upon
inquiring after him, I learned that he was amongst the
sick, and was very bad; but he was kindly attended by
the young man from the county Clare, who devoted himself to attending the afflicted, some of whom the members
of their own families neglected to take care of.

Sunday, June 20th.

Having hinted to the captain the propriety of having
divine service read upon the Sabbath, he said that it could
not be done. Indeed, the sailors seldom had a spare moment, and as to the mate, I often wondered how he got
through so much work. This day, therefore, had no mark

to distinguish it from any other. The poor emigrants
were in their usual squalid attire; neither did the crew
rig themselves out as on former Sundays.

All were dispirited, and a cloud of melancholy hung
over us.

The poor mistress deplored that she could not get an opportunity of reading her Bible. I pitied her from my
heart; knowing how much she felt the distress that surrounded us, and her anxiety to lighten the affliction of the
passengers.

Monday, June 21st.

I was surprised at the large allowance of food served out
to the sailors. They had each 1 1-2 lbs. of beef, or pork,
daily, besides coffee, and as much biscuit as they pleased;
but it being a temperance vessel, they had no grog,— in
lieu of which they got lime-juice. However, there was a
little cask of brandy in a corner of the cabin; but the captain was afraid to broach it, knowing the mate's propensi-
ty. I noticed the latter often casting a wistful glance at it
as he rose from dinner; and he did not fail to tell me that
it was the best possible preventive against the fever.

Tuesday, June 22nd.

One of the sailors was unable for duty, and the mate
feared he had the fever.

The reports from the hold were growing even more
alarming, and some of the patients who were mending, had
relapsed. One of the women was every moment expected
to breathe her last, and her friends, — an aunt and cousins,
— were inconsolable about her; as they persuaded her to
leave her father and mother, and come with them. The

mate said that her feet were swollen to double their natural size, and covered with black putrid spots. I spent a considerable part of the day watching a shark that followed in our wake with great constancy.

Wednesday, June 23d.

At breakfast I inquired of the mate after the young woman who was so ill yesterday, when he told me that she was dead; and when I remarked that I feared her burial would cause great consternation, I learned that the sad ordeal was over, her remains having been consigned to the deep within an hour after she expired. When I went on deck I heard the moans of her poor aunt, who continued to gaze upon the ocean as if she could mark the spot where the waters opened for their prey. The majority of the wretched passengers, who were not themselves ill, were absorbed in grief for their relatives; but some of them, it astonished me to perceive, had no feeling whatever, either for their fellow creatures' woe, or in the contemplation of being themselves overtaken by the dreadful disease. There was a further addition to the sick list, which now amounted to twenty.

Thursday, June 24th.

Being the festival of St. John, and a Catholic holiday, some young men and women got up a dance in the evening, regardless of the moans and cries of those who were tortured by the fiery fever. When the mate spoke to them of the impropriety of such conduct, they desisted and retired to the bow, where they sat down and spent the remainder of the evening singing. The monotonous howling they kept up was quite in unison with the scene of desolation within, and the dreary expanse of ocean without.

Friday, June 25th.   43 deg. 24 min. N. lat., 40 deg. 4 min. W. lon.

This morning there was a further accession to the names upon the sick roll.   It was awful how suddenly some were stricken.   A little child who was playing with its companions, suddenly fell down, and for some time was sunk in a death-like torpor, from which, when she awoke, she commenced to scream violently, and writhed in convulsive agony.   A poor woman who was warming a drink at the fire for her husband, also dropped down quite senseless, and was borne to her berth.

I found it very difficult to acquire precise information respecting the progressive symptoms of the disease, the different parties of whom I inquired disagreeing in some particulars ; but I inferred that the first symptom was generally a reeling in the head, followed by a swelling pain, as if the head were going to burst.   Next came excruciating pains in the bones, and then a swelling of the limbs, commencing with the feet, in some cases ascending the body, and again descending before it reached the head, stopping at the throat. The period of each stage varied in different patients; some of whom were covered with yellow, watery pimples, and others with red and purple spots, that turned into putrid sores.

Saturday, June 26th.   44 deg. 21 min. N. lat., 41 deg. 36 min. W. lon.

Some of those who the other day appeared to bid defiance to the fever, were seized in its relentless grasp; and a few who were on the recovery, relapsed.   It seemed miraculous to me that such subjects could struggle with so violent a disease without any effective aid.

Sunday, June 27th.   44 deg. 9 min. N. lat., 42 deg. 10 min. W. lon.

The moaning and raving of the patients kept me awake

nearly all the night; and I could hear the mistress stirring about until a late hour. It made my heart bleed to listen to the cries for " Water, for God's. sake some water." Oh! it was horrifying; yet, strange to say, I had no fear of taking the fever, which, perhaps, under the merciful providence of the Almighty, was a preventive cause. The mate, who spent much of his time among the patients, described to me some revolting scenes he witnessed in the hold; but they were too disgusting to be repeated. He became very much frightened, and often looked quite bewildered.

Monday, June 28th.

The number of patients upon the list now amounted to thirty, and the effluvium of the hold was shocking.

The passengers suffered much for want of pure water, and the mate tried the quality of all the casks. Fortunately he discovered a few which were better, and this circumstance was rather cheering.

Tuesday, June 29th. 43 deg. 24 min. N. lat., 46 deg. 37 min. W. lon.

The wind kept us to the south, but though occasionally becalmed, we were slowly gaining longitude.

I could not keep my mind fixed upon a book, so I was obliged to give over reading, and spent the day watching the rolling of the dolphin, the aerial darts of the flying-fish, with the gambols of numbers of porpoises that danced in the waters around the prow. It being the mate's watch, I remained upon deck until midnight, listening to his yarns. Some of them were rather incredible, and upon expressing such to be my opinion, he was inclined to take offence. Being the hero of some of his stories himself, I could not doubt the veracity of them, though they were not the least marvellous. Although a well informed and intelligent

man, he was very superstitious. But it is not uncommon
for sailors to be so.

Wednesday, June 30th. 43 deg. 48 min. N. lat., 48 deg. 6 min. W. lon.

Passing the main hatch, I got a glimpse of one of the
most awful sights I ever beheld. A poor female patient
was lying in one of the upper berths — dying. Her head
and face were swollen to a most unnatural size ; the latter
being hideously deformed. I recollected remarking the
clearness of her complexion when I saw her in health,
shortly after we sailed. She then was a picture of good
humor and contentment ; now, how sadly altered! Her
cheeks retained their ruddy hue, but the rest of her distorted
countenance was of a leprous whiteness. She had been
nearly three weeks ill, and suffered exceedingly until the
swelling set in, commencing in her feet, and creeping up
her body to her head. Her afflicted husband stood by her
holding a " blessed candle" in his hand, and awaiting the
departure of her spirit. Death put a period to her existence
shortly after I saw her. And as the sun was setting, the
bereaved husband muttered a prayer over her enshrouded
corpse, which, as he said " Amen," was lowered into the
ocean.

Thursday, July 1st. 44 deg. 36 min. N. lat., 48 deg. 38 min. W. lon.

The wind was still unfavorable, but we gained a little
by constantly tacking, and were approaching the banks of
Newfoundland. Some new cases were announced, making thirty-seven now lying. A convalescent was assisted
on deck, and seemed revived by the fresh air. He was a
miserable object. His face being yellow and withered,
was rendered ghastly by the black streak that encircled his
sunken eyes

CHAPTER V.

About midnight the shipmen deemed that they drew near to some country, and sounded. — ACTS OF THE APOSTLES.

Friday, July 2nd.

WE were enveloped in a dense fog, and had a horn sounding constantly. One of the patients, who was represented to be dying, sent for the mate, and giving him the key of his box, in which there was a small sum of money, requested him to take charge of it, and, upon his return to Ireland, send it to his (the sick man's) mother.

The mate promised to do so, but did not consider the poor fellow as bad as he himself feared he was.

Saturday, July 3d.

Any idea I ever formed of complete horror, was excelled by the stern reality of the frightful picture which the past night presented. The gloom spread around by the impenetrable fog was heightened by the dismal tone of the fog-horn, between each sound of which might be heard the cries and ravings of the delirious patients, and occasionally the tolling of a bell, warning us of the vicinity of some fishing-boat, numbers of which were scattered over the banks. The mate being unable to make an observation, we were obliged to depend upon his "dead reckoning."

Sunday, July 4th.

We enjoyed a favorable breeze, and the fog having

cleared off at noon, the mate had an observation, by which
we were in 45° 11' N. lat., 51° 40' W. lon. No new cases
of sickness were reported, but some of the patients were
said to be very bad.

We spoke a bark and a brig, both homeward bound;
and differed but little in longitude. There was something
exciting in listening to the friendly voice from the deep
toned speaking-trumpet, and in beholding the board
marked with the longitude. In a few moments the ensigns
were lowered, and each pursued its course.

The day was exceedingly cold; so much so, that the
captain supposed that we were in the neighbourhood of
icebergs; and I hoped to see one of these castellated floating masses, lifting its pinnacles on high, and glittering in
the rays of the sun.

Monday, July 5th.   45 deg. 21 min. N. lat., 53 deg. 52 min. W. lon.

The morning was foggy, and we were near running
into a French fishing-boat.

The captain having given orders for sounding, Jack was
sent to find the reel and line, which he brought up from
the depths of the lazaretto. This receptacle for all sorts of
commodities was situated below the cabin; and it afforded
me some amusement to see the boy, by the faint light of
the lantern, groping among beef casks, pork barrels, paint
and tar pots, spars, and rusty irons. The sails having
been put aback, so that the brig stood motionless upon the
bosom of the water, the reel was held by a man at the
stern, and the line being uncoiled, was drawn outside the
ropes of the rigging, until it reached the bow. The lead
was then attached, and carried by a seaman to the point of

the bowsprit, where the sailor sat swinging the weight, like a pendulum, until, upon the order to heave, he cast it forth upon its mission. Bottom having been found at thirty-four fathoms, the line was placed upon a pulley and drawn up; when there was found imbedded in the grease with which the lead was filled, fine white sand, as laid down in the chart.

The sails were again set to the breeze, and we were once more gliding through the water, the momentary commotion soon settling down into the usual inanity.

Tuesday, July 6th. 45 deg. 37 min. N. lat., 54 deg. 53 min. W. lon. 7 deg.

During the past night there was a heavy fall of rain, which left the atmosphere clear and cool.

Two men (brothers) died of dysentery, and I was awakened by the noise made by the mate, who was searching for an old sail to cover the remains with. In about an hour after, they were consigned to the deep, a remaining brother being the solitary mourner. He continued long to gaze upon the ocean, while a tear that dropped from his moistened eye told the grief he did not otherwise express. I learned in the afternoon that he was suffering from the same complaint that carried off his brothers.

Wednesday, July 7th.

The phosphorescent appearance of the ocean at night was very beautiful. We seemed to be gliding through a sea of liquid fire. We passed a great number of fishing-boats, chiefly French, from the isles Miquelon and St. Pierre.

They were anchored at regular intervals, for the purpose of catching cod-fish, which, allured by the vast numbers of worms found upon the bottom, abound upon the banks.

The vessels generally are large sloops, and have a platform all round, with an awning over the deck. When a fish is taken, it is immediately split and cleaned; then it is thrown into the hold; and when the latter is full, the fishermen return home, and land their cargo, to be dried and saved·

Owing to these processes being sometimes too long deferred, the bank fish, though larger, is considered inferior to that taken along the coast of Newfoundland.

Great variety of opinion exists respecting the nature and origin of these submarine banks, but none of them appears to me so natural as this : — The stream which issues from the Gulf of Mexico, commonly called the "Florida gulf stream," being checked in its progress by the southern coast of Newfoundland, deposits the vast amount of matter held in suspension. This by accumulation formed the Banks, which are still increasing in extent. The temperature of the water upon the Banks is higher than that of the Gulf of St. Lawrence, and of the ocean; and its evaporation causes the fog that almost perpetually prevails.

The afternoon was clear, with a gentle breeze, which formed a ripple on the surface of the water, and gave a beautiful appearance to the reflection of the declining sun, looking like jets of gas bursting from the deep.

Thursday, July 8th.   45 deg. 24 min. N. lat., 57 deg. W. lon.

Another of the crew was taken ill, thereby reducing our hands when they were most required. The captain had a great dread of the coast of Newfoundland, which being broken into deep bays, divided from each other by rocky capes, is rendered exceedingly perilous; more especially, as the powerful currents set towards this inhospitable shore.

We kept a lookout for some vessel coming from the gulf, in order to learn the bearings of land, but did not perceive one during the day.

Friday, July 9th. 46 deg. N. lat., 58 deg. W. lon.

A few convalescents appeared upon deck. The appearance of the poor creatures was miserable in the extreme. We now had fifty sick, being nearly one half the whole number of passengers. Some entire families being prostrated, were dependent on the charity of their neighbours, many of whom were very kind; but others seemed to be possessed of no feeling. Among the former, the Headcommittee was conspicuous. The brother of the two men who died on the sixth instant, followed them to-day. He was seized with dismay from the time of their death, which no doubt hurried on the malady to its fatal termination. The old sails being all used up, his remains were placed in two meal-sacks, and a weight being fastened at foot, the body was placed upon one of the hatch battens, from which, when raised over the bulwark, it fell into the deep, and was no more seen. He left two little orphans, one of whom, a boy seven years of age, I noticed in the evening, wearing his deceased father's coat. Poor little fellow! he seemed quite unconscious of his loss, and proud of the accession to his scanty covering. The remainder of the man's clothes were sold by auction, by a friend of his who promised to take care of the children. There was great competition, and the " Cant," as they called it, occasioned jibing and jesting, which it was painful to listen to, surrounded as the actors were, (some of whom had just risen from a bed of sickness) by famine, pestilence and death.

CHAPTER VI.

The floods are risen, O Lord, the floods have lifted up their voice ; the floods lift up their waves. The waves of the sea are mighty and rage horribly : but yet the Lord who dwelleth on high is mightier. DAVID.

July 10th, 46 deg. 36 min. N. lat, 59 deg. 36 min. W. lon.

WE spoke a wherry which was conveying cattle from Nova Scotia to Newfoundland, and learned from the steersman the bearings of St. Paul's Island. We shortly afterwards passed a large fleet, coming from the gulf, and in the afternoon descried Cape North.

The passengers expressed great delight at seeing land, and were under the impression that they were near their destination, little knowing the extent of the gulf they had to pass, and the great river to ascend. Early in the evening we saw Isle St. Paul, and indistinctly the point of Cape Ray, between which and Cape North is the passage into the Gulf, of St. Lawrence. St. Paul's Island lies about ten miles to the north of the latter cape, in latitude 47° 14' north, and longitude 60° 11' 17" west. It is a huge rock, dividing at top into three conical peaks. Rising boldly from the sea, there is a great depth of water all round it, and vessels may pass at either side of it, It has been the site of numerous shipwrecks ; many vessels, carried out of their reckoning by the currents, having been dashed against it when concealed by fog, and instantly shattered to atoms.

Human bones and other memorials of these disasters are strewed around its base. We passed the light of this dangerous island, at 10 p. m., entering into the "goodly, great gulf, full of islands, passages, and entrances, towards what wind soever you please to bend." *

This gulf was first explored by John Cabot, in 1497, who called the coast of Labrador *Primavista.* The Portuguese afterwards changed the name of that desert region to Terra Coterealis; and the gulf they designated as that of the "Two Brothers," in memory of Gaspar and Michael Cotereal, the first named of whom not having returned from the second expedition he commanded, the latter went in search of him; but neither of them were afterwards heard of.

Jaques Cartier having entered it upon the festival of St. Lawrence, gave to the gulf and the river flowing into it the name they still retain.

Sunday, July 11th.

We had a fair wind, and were going full sail at 7 knots an hour. At noon we passed the Bird Islands, which are low ledges of rocks, and swarm with gannets, numbers of which were flying about. They were as large as geese, and pure white with the exception of the tips of the wings, which were jet black. Some of Mother Carey's chickens were following in our wake, and it was highly amusing to watch the contentions of the little creatures for bits of fat thrown to them.

We had a distant view of the Magdalen Islands, which, although lying nearer to Nova Scotia, are considered as

* Cartier.

belonging to Canada; and form a portion of the circuit within the district of Gaspé, a court being held at Amherst harbor annually, from 1st to 10th of July. The largest of the group are Bryon, Deadman's, Amherst, Entry, and Wolf islands, which are inhabited by a hardy race of fishermen. The huge walrus may at times be seen upon their shores.

Monday, July 12th.

In the morning we were becalmed, the water being smooth as glass, and of a beautifully clear, green hue.

A breeze sprung up at 12 o'clock, and the captain having provided himself and me with lines, we spent the afternoon fishing for mackerel, which were so plenty that I caught seventy in about two hours, when I had to give over, my hands being cut by the line. The captain continued, and had a barrel full by evening. They were the finest mackerel I ever saw, and we had some at tea, which we all enjoyed as a delicious treat after six weeks of salt beef and biscuit diet. Many of the passengers having noticed our success, followed our example, and lines were out from every quarter; all the twine, thread, &c. that could be made out, being put into requisition, with padlocks and bolts for weights, and wire hooks. Even with such rude gear, they caught a great number; but their recreation was suddenly terminated, a young man who was drawing in a fish having dropped upon the deck quite senseless, and apparently dead. He was carried below and put into his berth, there to pass through the successive stages of the fever.

Tuesday, July 13th.

We were again becalmed during the forenoon, but a

breeze that soon became a gale arose about one o'clock, p.
m., and lasted until evening, being accompanied by thunder and lightning, and followed by a heavy shower of rain.
The clouds cleared away at sunset, when we were within
10 or 12 miles of the eastern point of the island of Anticosti,
which when the captain perceived, he gave the order to
sheer off on the other tack. This island is particularly
dangerous, being surrounded by sunken reefs. It is of
considerable extent, being 130 miles in length from east to
west, and 30 miles across its greatest breadth. Its surface
is low and level, and covered with a pristine forest, through
which prowls the bear, undisturbed, except when hunted
by Indians, who periodically resort hither for that purpose.

The sterility of its soil offering no inducement to the
white man, it is uninhabited, except by the keepers of the
lighthouses, to which are attached small establishments
for the purpose of affording relief to shipwrecked mariners.
The name Anticosti is probably a corruption of Natiscotee,
which it is called by the aborigines. Cartier named it
" L'isle de l'Assumption.

Wednesday, July 14th.

We had the bold headlands of capes Gaspé and Rosier
on our left, and had entered the majestic river St. Lawrence,
which here, through a mouth ninety miles in width, after
a course of upwards of 2,000 miles, disgorges the accumulated waters of the great lakes, swollen by the accession of hundreds of tributaries, (some of them noble rivers,)
draining an almost boundless region.

The reports of the sufferings in the hold were heart-
rending. Simon and Jack were both taken ill.

Thursday, July 15th.

Last night I was suddenly wakened by the captain, shouting "get up! get up! and come on deck quickly." Somewhat alarmed, I obeyed the summons as speedily as possible, and was well recompensed for the start, by the magnificence of the glorious scene I beheld. The northern portion of the firmament was vividly illuminated with a clear though subdued light, while across it shot fiery meteors from different directions; now rushing against each other as if engaged in deadly warfare; again gliding about in wanton playfulness.

Disappearing for a while, and leaving behind a faintly luminous trail, they would again burst forth upon their stage, lighted up by a sudden flash for the igneous performers. I watched with delight until the lustrous picture was finally enshrouded in darkness, when I returned to bed.

There was a birth on board this morning, and two or three deaths were momentarily expected. The mate's account of the state of the hold was harrowing. It required the greatest coercion to enforce any thing like cleanliness or decency; and the Head committee had no sinecure office. I spent the greater part of the day upon deck, admiring the numberless jets d'eau of the bottlenosed whales that plunged about in the water. The poor mistress was greatly grieved about Jack and Simon; and the captain was savage for lack of assistance.

Friday, July 16th.

We were tacking about all day, which though tedious I enjoyed, as it afforded an opportunity of seeing both shores of the noble river. That to the north is indescribably grand; rugged mountains rising precipitously from out the water,

and indented by sweeping bays, in which are numerous
islets. Towards evening we were in view of Seven Islands
bay, lovely though desolate. No human eyes behold this
region of unbroken solitude, save now and then those which
can but lightly appreciate its grandeur. - I cannot describe
the effect produced by the mist that sometimes completely
hides the mountains — rolling up their sides, and resembling gracefully festooned drapery.

The sailors who could work were greatly harassed by
being obliged to tack repeatedly. The mate, especially,
was one moment down in the hold waiting on some dying
fellow-creature; the next, perhaps, stretched across a yard,
reefing a top-sail. Although lame, he was surprisingly active, and used to astonish the emigrants, one of whom said
to me, " Och! your honor, isn't Mister Mate a great bit of
a man ? "

Saturday, July 17th.

The morning was fine, and shortly after breakfast I was
upon deck admiring the beauty of the pine-clad hills upon
the southern shore of the river, when the captain came up
from the cabin, and after looking about gave the word to
" double reef top-sails and make all snug." Not long
after, the sky, which had been quite clear, became black,
and a violent gale arose, lashing the water into tremendous
waves, which tossed us mercilessly about; one moment
borne up by an angry billow; the next, plunging into a
·deep abyss. The roaring wind was drowned by the tremendous noise of successive peals of thunder, while the
forked lightning played about in zig-zag lines, and the rain
descended in torrents.

At 5, P. M., the wind abated, and the waves began to

4

subside. About an hour after, the leaden clouds parted, and, as if in defiance of the contending elements, the sun set in gorgeous splendor. The poor passengers were greatly terrified by the storm, and suffered exceedingly. They were so buffetted about that the sick could not be tended; and after calm was restored a woman was found dead in her berth.

CHAPTER VII.

So frequent death,
Sorrow he more than causes, but confounds;
For human sighs, his rival strokes contend,
And make distress, distraction.
                                                    YOUNG.

Sunday, July 18th.

I was enchanted with the extraordinary beauty of the scenery I beheld this morning, when I came on deck. — The early beams of the sun played upon the placid surface of the river, here forty miles wide, the banks on either hand being moderately elevated, and covered with firs. On the north was Cape des Monts, terminating in a low point, on which stood a light-house and diminutive cottage. On the south Cape Chat rose to a considerable height; the outline of its summit being broken by sudden gaps, giving to it a character that to me was unique.

An unbroken stillness reigned around, as if nature were at rest after the storm of the previous day; and our brig lay almost motionless upon the water.

I occupied myself again and again noting, so as to impress upon my mind, the peerless beauty I am unable to portray, and in reading the Acts of the Apostles. I felt a renewed interest in the account of St. Paul's voyages, as I could now appreciate by experience the force and accuracy of their description. We made no way, and it was with difficulty we retained our position against the current.

Monday, July 19th.

Another death and burial. A few who had been ill, again appeared on deck, weak, and weary. The want of pure water was sensibly felt by the afflicted creatures, and we were yet a long way from where the river loses its saltness. In the morning there came alongside of us a beautiful little schooner, from which we took a pilot on board. When he found that we had emigrants, and so much sickness, he seemed to be frightened and disappointed; as he had avoided a large ship, thinking we had not passengers. However, he could not nor dare he retreat. The first thing he did was to open his huge trunk, and take from it a pamphlet, which proved to be the quarantine regulations; he handed it to the captain, who spent a long time poring over it. When he had read it I got a look at it — one side was printed in French, the other in English. The rules were very stringent, and the penalties for their infringement exceedingly severe; the sole control being vested in the head physician, the power given to whom was most arbitrary. We feared that we should undergo a long detention in quarantine, and learned that we could hold no communication whatever with the shore until our arrival at Grosse Isle.

The pilot was a heavy, stupid fellow — a Canadian, speaking a horrible patois, and broken English; he was accompanied by his nephew and apprentice, Pierre, a fine lad.

The wind favored us for some hours, and towards evening we saw Mount Camille upon the southern bank, rising above the surrounding hills to a height of 2036 feet.

Tuesday, July 20th.

Our course lying more to the southern bank of the river, I could observe minutely the principal objects upon that side. Many charming tributary streams rolled along sweet valleys, enfolded in the swelling hills, whose sides were clothed with verdure. I would fain explore each of these enchanting vales; but too soon we passed them, and some jutting cape would hide from view the little settlements at each embouchure. The most considerable of these, was that upon Point aux Snellez, near the mouth of the river Metis, about 200 miles from Quebec. Here commences the Kempt road, which terminates at Cross point on the river Restigouche,—a distance of 98 miles. A new road, connecting this with Grande Nouvelle on the Bay of Chaleur, completes the communication with Halifax.

Wednesday, July 21st.

A thick fog concealed every object from view, at times so low as only to hide the hulls of vessels, by whose rigging we could perceive them tacking like ourselves; the sky being unclouded. A strong wind blew down the river, which together with the forcible current kept us back. One of the sick sailors reappeared upon deck, but was too weak to resume duty; the other man was still very bad; as were also Simon and Jack.

Simon got up from his berth in a delirious fit, and ran down to the cabin, where his wild appearance nearly frightened the life out of the mistress. It was with difficulty he was laid hold of; and he resisted violently while he was carried back to his hammock, in the forecastle, where he was strapped down.

Thursday, July 22nd.

Soon after retiring to my berth last night, I heard a grating noise, accompanied by a tremulous motion of the brig, and felt alarmed, fearing that we had grounded upon some bank; but my anxiety was relieved, by learning that it was caused by the dropping of the anchor, it being useless to contend against both wind and current. The latter here being strengthened by the vast body of water discharged from the river Saguenay. When I came on deck this morning, I found that we were anchored off the village of Trois Pistolles, with Cape L'Orignal to the east, and Basque Isle on the west. Being the first Canadian village I had seen, I was delighted by the rural aspect of the pretty white cottages with red roofs, scattered over the sloping bank, each surrounded by a small garden. The captain was impatient, and though the pilot said it would only tend to harass the sailors, we weighed anchor at noon, and after beating about all the day, again came to, near the same spot as before. A child, one of the orphans, died and was buried in the evening, no friend being by to see the frail body committed to its watery grave. The water could not be used by the wretched emigrants, and but half a cask of that provided for the cabin and crew remained; they were therefore obliged to use the saline water of the river.

Friday, July 23d.

We remained at anchor all day, a fresh breeze blowing down the river. Some of the recovered patients who were slowly regaining strength, had relapsed into the most violent stages, and three new cases were announced, showing exceedingly virulent symptoms.

The wind abated at noon, and it was quite calm for about an hour. During this period I was upon deck, and on looking across the river was greatly astonished at perceiving something resembling an island, which I had not before noticed. It was circular, and quite black. I spent some time in conjecturing what it could be; the captain could not tell; and the pilot was asleep. At length two vessels sailing down the river, when they came near this object, assumed a similar appearance, from which I immediately inferred that it was a ship at anchor, transformed by mirage.

As the vessels sailed along, they underwent extraordinary metamorphoses — sometimes the bow and stern were turned up like those of a Chinese junk; at others the hulls were up in the air and the masts seemingly in the water; the latter being twisted and curved. A cottage upon the north bank stood apparently upon the surface of the river, and the light-house on Bic island had a duplicate of itself perched upon it, the copy being inverted, lantern down and base up. The illusions occurred only within certain limits, which were defined by an appearance distinct from the surrounding atmosphere. The difference being something like that presented by clear water and the empty space within a half filled vial.

CHAPTER VIII.

These are miracles, which man,
Cag'd in the bounds of Europe's pigmy plan,
Can scarcely dream of; which his eye must see,
To know how beautiful this world can be.   MOORE.

Saturday, July 24th.

WE once more weighed anchor this morning, and beat
about all the day between Trois Pistolles and the mouth
of the river Escamin, which discharges itself nearly opposite,
upon the north shore. We had a large fleet of ships,
barques, and brigs in company, two of which were trans-
ports with troops. It was a pleasing sight to see such a
number of vessels, continually passing each other, and
each evidently endeavoring to gain upon the rest, every
tack.

In the afternoon a brig hoisted her ensign as a signal of
recognition, and upon the next tack we passed near enough
to speak; when the captain turned out to be a particular
friend of our captain and the mistress. They kept up a
regular conversation the rest of the day, every time we
met, which was pretty often; each inquiring of the other,
the number of deaths? — what sickness? — how many
days out? — from what port? &c. &c. We learned, much
to our surprise, that she had a greater number of
deaths than we; and this news was very consoling to the
mistress. Towards evening the wind abated, and we were
in hope that it was about to change. It died away alto-

gether, and the vessels that before shot past one another, were now almost motionless, and scattered over the surface of the river, which here is twenty-five miles wide. At sunset we lay at the north side, and could almost reach the trees covering the bank. I have seen many a beautiful sunset, but all fade before the exquisite beauty of that which I witnessed this evening. The glorious luminary sunk behind the dark blue hills, upon the summits of which seemed to rest the border of heaven's canopy, dyed in crimson sheen, softening down to a light orange tint, that imperceptibly blended with the azure sky, which was here and there hid by fleecy vermilion clouds. Cape L' Orignal was clothed in a vesture of purple, of every shade, from violet to that of the deepest hue, o'ershadowing the village of Trois Pistolles. There was not a ripple upon the water, but gentle undulations heaved its bosom, decked in a tissue of carmine, ultramarine, and gold. Such vividness and variety of colors I never before conceived, or since experienced. Oh! thought I, why is not Danby here to fix them upon imperishable canvass? As night came on the pilot grew uneasy, there not being good anchorage at that side; however, a slight breeze from the old quarter wafted us across, to the very spot where we before lay, and where we again dropped anchor in the midst of our consorts.

Sunday, July 25th.

We lay at anchor all day, the wind blowing strongly against us. It was exceedingly trying to be detained here within a few miles of the tidal influence, having once gained which, we would be independent of the wind. The poor patients, too, were anxiously looking out for the quar

4*

antine station, where they hoped to find some alleviation to their sufferings. The mistress and mate were uneasy, as the cabin water was nearly out, and they feared to let the captain know of it. I was obliged to remain below, the effluvia from the hold being quite overpowering. I could hear the tolling of the village church-bell, and its sweet tone induced me to go on deck for a few moments, where I was charmed with the appearance of the showily dressed Canadians, some standing in groups, talking; others seated upon benches, while caleshes were momentarily arriving with "habitans" from distant settlements, who, after tying up their horses under a shed close by the "presbytere," joined the chatting parties until the bell ceased, when all retired within the church.

Monday, July 26th.

The wind was not so strong, and the effluvia not quite so unpleasant. I was therefore not so much confined to the cabin. The captain was desirous of sailing, but the pilot would not consent; and the latter proved to be right, as two of the vessels weighed anchor in the morning, and after beating about for a couple of hours were obliged to come to. A pretty stream, — the mingled waters of the Abawisquash and Trois Pistolles rivers, — flows into the St. Lawrence, adjacent to the village. Like all the tributaries upon the southern side, it is of inconsiderable length, the hills in which they have their sources lying at no great distance from the bank. But many of those which empty themselves at the north side, as the Manicouagan, Bustard, Belsiamites, Portneuf, &c., are fine rivers, rising in the elevated ridge that divides Canada from the Hudson's Bay territory; and in their courses through the untrodden forests expanding into large lakes. After dinner the mistress carried the baby that was born on board, down to the cabin. The captain at first was very angry; but a smile upon the face of the little innocent, softened his heart, and he soon caressed it with all the endearments he was in the habit of lavishing upon the canary; when tired of which amusement, he opened 'the locker and took therefrom an egg, which he held up to the light and looked through, to see if it were good. Not being satisfied on that point, he tried another, and then another, until he got one to please him. He next got some salt, and opening the infant's little hand, placed it upon the palm, and gently closed the tiny fingers upon it. He then performed a similar operation upon the other, enclosing a shilling in lieu of salt. The egg he handed to the mistress to send to the mother, and acquaint her that he wished the child to be called "Ellen," after her.

The mistress, kind to all, was particularly so to the little children, about twenty of whom we had aboard. One poor infant, whose father and mother (neither of whom were twenty years of age) were both ill and unable to take care of it, she paid a woman for nursing; and I could not believe it to be the same child when I saw it clean and comfortably covered with clothes she made for it. Jack came upon deck. Poor fellow! he was sadly altered. Simon also was reported to be better, but unable to leave his hammock. The mate began to complain, and the brandy cask, (which had been broached,) supplied his remedy.

Tuesday, July 27th.

The wind veered about five o'clock last evening, and the

vessels, one by one, sailed away. Our pilot saying that it would again change in a short time, was not inclined to weigh anchor, but the captain insisted upon doing so. At 6 p. m. we were once more in motion, and in a few minutes were in full sail, going seven knots an hour. Basque island was soon left behind, and stemming the dark waters discharged by the Saguenay, as day was fading, we were before Tadousac, a settlement at the mouth of that grand river. The Saguenay ranks second amongst the tributaries of the St. Lawrence; indeed, although its course is not so long, it is supposed to convey a larger body of water than the Ottawa. At its juncture with the St. Lawrence it is about a mile wide; but in some parts it expands to three. At a distance of one hundred and forty miles it receives the waters of lake St. John, which is the reservoir of numerous rivers, some of which are precipitated into it by magnificent rapids and falls. This lake, which is about one hundred miles in circumference, is remarkable for its shallowness, from which cause the navigation of it is frequently dangerous; as the least wind produces a ground swell and breakers. Its water is said to be tepid, and it abounds with a variety of fish, great quantities of which are taken at the mouth of the Ouiatchouan river, where there is a station, at which they are salted and packed for traffic. The climate is very salubrious, and the soil of the great valley that borders the lake is susceptible of the highest culture. A few Indians wander over this fine tract of country, which it is the intention of the provincial government to open to French Canadians, whose laws acknowledging no right of primogeniture, they have overpopulated many of the old settlements. The Indians call this fine

sheet of water, "Piegougamis," signifying "the flat lake."
First-class ships can ascend the Saguenay to Chicoutimi,
a distance of sixty-eight miles. There is a small settlement here, the communication between which and the
lake, being broken by rapids, can only be overcome by experienced "voyageurs" in canoes. At Ha-Ha Bay, eigh-
teen miles below Chicoutimi, there is a pretty large settlement, and here the river assumes its grand and romantic
feature, passing for the remainder of its course between
almost perpendicular cliffs, from one thousand to fifteen
hundred feet in height. Its great depth is another charac-
teristic; bottom not being found near the mouth with a
line of three hundred and thirty fathoms; while the depth
of the St. Lawrence at the junction is but two hundred and
forty feet. However, its great rapidity renders it impossi-
ble accurately to learn its soundings.

CHAPTER IX.

But soft! the tinges of the west decline,
And night falls dewy o'er these banks of pine.
Among the reeds in which our idle boat
Is rock'd to rest, the wind's complaining note
Dies, like a half breath'd whispering of flutes.
Along the waves the gleaming porpoise shoots,
And I can trace him like a wat'ry star,
Down the steep current, till he fades afar
Amid the foaming breakers' silvery light,
Where yon rough rapids sparkle through the night.—MOORE.

July 27th.

FEELING somewhat excited by the sudden acceleration
of our progress, I determined to remain on deck until the
turn of the tide would compel us to come to an anchor.
There was something also most enchanting in being wafted by both wind and tide, at the rate of ten knots an hour,
watching the lights upon the different islands, and the
myriads of bright stars that studded the firmament, and
were reflected in the darkened surface of the broad river,
which upon the north side was overshadowed by the
mountainous banks, while the southern shore might be
traced by a continuous line of flickering lamps within the
cottages upon its border. We soon left Green island behind us; then Hare island and Riviere du Loup, upon
which is a large settlement with a population of about fifteen hundred. There are some large saw-mills here, and
a "portage" leading through Madawaska to the lower
provinces. After passing the Pilgrims, a group of rocky

islets, I went below, and had not long " turned in" when I heard and felt the dropping of the anchor.

In the morning I found that we lay off Kamouraska, which is charmingly situated in a rich district, at the base of a chain of hills that rise behind the village, and stretch far beyond it. This lovely spot, being one of the healthiest places in Lower Canada, attracts many visitors during the summer season. It is also enriched by the fisheries established upon the numerous islands that lie immediately in front, supplying abundance of shad, salmon, herrings, &c. Directly opposite, upon the other side of the river, is Murray Bay, into which flows the Malbaie River, upon whose banks reside the descendants of Wolfe's highlanders, many of whom settled there, after the campaign. The bay is environed by an amphitheatre of majestic hills, cultivated to the very summits, their sloping sides being dotted over with comfortable abodes.

We weighed anchor at noon, and gently glided through a scene of indescribable loveliness. The noble river here unbroken by islands, presented a lake-like expanse, bounded by the lofty Cap Diable, and Goose Cape. Village succeeded village upon the south shore; and the gigantic hills upon the north were adorned by sweet alpine cots, surrounded by cleared patches of land, embosomed by the dark green pines. The weather was very warm, and nature basked in uninterrupted sunshine. Oh! what a contrast to this magic beauty was presented within our floating pest-house; not that matters were worse than they had been; there was rather an abatement in the violence of the fever, and I perceived some faces, that I with difficulty recognized, so changed were they since I saw them, before their illness. Simon and Jack were both on deck, the former being deprived of memory, and partially deranged in his mind. Poor fellow! having, the previous voyage, fallen from the topsail yard, and injured his head, his intellect was thereby impaired, and the fever confirmed the insanity, which had not left him when I quitted the brig, some three weeks after. Being now in fresh water the passengers were relieved of one calamity, and the women who were able, were busy washing; two or three men were also similarly engaged, their wives being unable; and we endeavoured to impress upon them the fact, that the length of our detention in quarantine would greatly depend on the cleanliness of their persons, and of the hold. There were still some very bad cases, and the poor Head committee was in great trouble about his wife, who was dying. The mate still kept up, being afraid of going to hospital, but it was quite evident that he was very ill indeed.

We passed two steamers that were going down the river to tow up ships. We also had a Scotch brig, the " Delta," in company.

At 6 p. m., the tide being on the ebb, we once more anchored, opposite to the Isle aux Coudres, which lies in front of St. Paul's bay. This beautiful island was so named by Cartier, who found upon it a profusion of filberts. A smaller island lies inside of it, whose origin is thus accounted for in a manuscript belonging to the Jesuit college of Quebec; which relates the effects of the earthquake felt throughout Canada in 1663 : — "Near St. Paul's bay (fifty miles below Quebec, on the north side,) a mountain about a quarter of a league in circumference, situated on the shore of the St. Lawrence, was precipitated into the river; but, as if it had only made a plunge, it rose from the bottom and became a small island, forming with the shore a convenient harbour, well sheltered from all winds." The same authority says, " Lower down the river, towards Point Alouettes, an entire forest of considerable extent was loosened from the main bank, and slid into the river St. Lawrence, where the trees took fresh root."

The rivers Du Gouffre and Des Marees empty themselves into St. Paul's bay, flowing through luxuriant valleys, intervening between the detached mountains.

Delightfully located upon an eminence, on the south bank, stands the village of St. Anne, at the head of a bay of the same name, into which flows the river Ouelle. It is large, and has a Catholic College, and some handsome churches.

The surrounding country is highly cultivated, presenting every feature of softness and beauty that can adorn a landscape.

The evening was a charming one,—clear and still,—the water smooth as a mirror, in which gleamed the reflection of the tin covered roofs and spires, that glittered in the rays of the setting sun; while occasionally a huge snow-white porpoise rose above the surface, plunging again beneath the water, which closing, formed circles, becoming larger and larger, until the unwieldy creature again appeared and formed them anew. I remained on deck long after all had retired to rest, and watched the gray twilight creeping over day, until it was illumined by the pale moon, which soon smiled upon one of earth's most beauteous pictures.

I retired to my berth, and took a short repose; which was broken shortly after midnight by the weighing of the

anchor. As I wished not to lose the sight of the least
part of the river (which I loved to look upon by night as
well as by day), I hurried on deck.

We passed through the Traverse — an intricate channel,
marked by floating lights — and by the Pillars, a group of
dangerous rocks on one of which is a revolving light. At
day-break we were passing Goose island, which at low
water is connected with Crane island, on the northern
extremity of which is the handsome residence of the sei-
gneur. The southern bank presented the same charming features, and in the distance I discerned the chain of
hills claimed by the United States as the boundary of the
State of Maine. In a short time we arrived before the
village of St. Thomas, picturesquely situated on the banks
of Riviere du Sud, in which were anchored some vessels
which were being freighted with lumber from the several
saw-mills. The soil in this neighbourhood is exceedingly
productive, and is well cultivated ; on which account it is
called the granary of the lower province. The village is
of considerable extent, and is composed of white houses,
clustering around a pretty church. A few miles further
sail brought us among a number of beautiful islets — so
beautiful that they seemed like a fairy scene ; their verdant
turf was almost level with the blue water that wound
amongst them, submerging not a few, so that the first that
grew upon them appeared to rise from the river. A vast
fleet of vessels lying at anchor told that we had arrived at
Grosse Isle ; and after wending our way amongst isles
and ships, we dropped anchor in the ground allotted for
vessels upon arrival, and hoisted our ensign at the peak,
as a signal for the inspecting physician to board us.

CHAPTER X.

And when I looked, behold, an hand was sent unto me; and, lo, a roll of a book was therein;
And he spread it before me; and it was written within and without; and there was written therein, lamentations, and mourning, and woe. — EZEKIEL.

Grosse Isle, July 28th.

By 6. A. M., we were settled in our new position before the quarantine station. The passengers that were able to be up were all busy, cleaning and washing, some clearing the hold of filth, others assisting the sailors in swabbing the deck. The mistress herself washed out the cabin last evening, and put every thing in order.

The captain commenced shaving himself at 7, and completed the operation in about an hour and a half. The mate was unable to do anything, but kept repeatedly calling to the mistress for brandy, and requested that his illness should be kept from the doctor, as he was sure he had not fever. Breakfast was speedily despatched, and anxiety was depicted on every countenance. At 9 o'clock a boat was perceived pulling towards us, with four oars and a steersman with a broad leafed straw hat and leather coat, who the pilot told us was the inspecting physician. In a few minutes the boat was alongside, and the doctor on deck. He hastily enquired for the captain, and before he could be answered was down in the cabin where the mistress was finishing her toilet. Having introduced himself, he enquired if we had sickness aboard ? — Its nature ? — How

many deaths? — How many patients at present? These
questions being answered, and the replies noted upon his
tablet, he snatched up his hat, — ran up the ladder, — along
the deck, — and down into the hold. Arrived there, "ha!"
said he, sagaciously, "there is fever here." He stopped
beside the first berth in which a patient was lying, — felt
his pulse, — examined his tongue, — and ran up the ladder
again. As he passed by me he handed me some papers
to be filled up by the captain, and to have ready "to-
morrow or next day." In an instant he was in his boat,
from which, while the men were taking up their oars, he
shouted out to me that I was not obliged to remain in
quarantine, and might go up to Quebec when I pleased.
I brought the papers to the captain, who remained in the
cabin, supposing that the doctor would return thither, in
order to give directions for our guidance; and when he
learned that that gentleman had gone, he was desperately
enraged. The mistress endeavored to pacify him by sug-
gesting that it was likely he would visit us again in the course
of the day, or at least that he would send a message to us.
When I acquainted the mistress that I was at liberty to leave
the brig, she looked at me most pitifully, as if she would say,
"Are you too going to desert us." But I had no such intention, and was determined to remain with them, at all
events until they reached Quebec. The poor passengers
expecting that they would be all reviewed, were dressed in
their best clothes, and were clean, though haggard and
weak. They were greatly disappointed in their expecta-
tions, as they were under the impression that the sick would
be immediately admitted to the hospital, and the healthy
landed upon the island, there to remain until taken to

Quebec by a steamer. Indeed, such was the procedure to be inferred from the book of directions given to the captain by the pilot, when he came aboard.

When the mistress appeared on deck, I scarcely knew her. She usually wore a black stuff gown, a red worsted "bosom friend," which she told me (at least once a day,) was knit for her by her neice; — with a cap having three full borders, which projected beyond the leaf of the little straw bonnet, covered with the accumulated stains and smoke of many a voyage. Now, she had on a new fancy striped calico dress, as showy as deep reds, yellows, blues and greens could make it, — a black satin bonnet, with no lack of red ribands, and a little conservatory of artificials around her good natured face, — not forgetting her silver spectacles. All day long we kept looking out for a message from shore, and in watching the doctor's boat, going from vessel to vessel; his visit to each occupying about the same time as to us, which was exactly five minutes. We sometimes fancied that he was making for us, but the boat the next moment would be concealed by some large ship; then we were sure we would be the next; but no, the rowers pulled for shore. The day wore away before we gave up hope.

I could not believe it possible, that here within reach of help we should be left as neglected as when upon the ocean; — that after a voyage of two months' duration, we were to be left still enveloped by reeking pestilence, the sick without medicine, medical skill, nourishment, or so much as a drop of pure water; for the river although not saline here, was polluted by the most disgusting objects, thrown overboard from the several vessels. In short, it was a floating mass of filthy straw, the refuse of foul beds, barrels containing the vilest matter, old rags, and tattered clothes, &c., &c. The Head committee was greatly grieved for his wife, whose death he momentarily expected. He had looked anxiously forward to the time when we should arrive here, hoping that at least the doctor would see her; but his hopes, as well as those of others, were suddenly blasted. The brig that arrived with us sailed for Quebec immediately after the doctor's visit, possibly not having had any sickness: five other vessels also were discharged. How long they were detained, we could not tell; but the captain was so provoked, that he vowed he would sail without permission. The pilot, who did not well understand his hasty disposition, ventured to remonstrate with him, and fell in for a hurricane of curses and abuse; to which, though ignorant of many of the expressions, he replied in French, not finding himself sufficiently eloquent in the English tongue.

Four vessels arrived with the evening tide, and hoisted their signals, but were not visited. Several sailed by us without stopping, not having passengers, and a vast number went down the river during the day. Two huge steamers also arrived, and in the afternoon brought off hundreds of human beings from the island.

Thursday, July 29th.

This morning a boat was perceived making towards us, which at first was thought to be the doctor's; but when it approached nearer there appeared but two persons in it, both of whom were rowing. In a few minutes more the boat was alongside, and from the cassocks and bands of the two gentlemen we learned that they were Canadian priests. They came on deck, each carrying a large black bag. They inquired for the captain, who received them courteously, and introduced them to the mistress and to me, after which they conversed awhile in French with the pilot, whom they knew; when, having put on their vestments, they descended into the hold. They there spent a few minutes with each of the sick, and administered the last rites to the dying woman and an old man, terminating their duties by baptizing the infant. They remained in the hold for about an hour, and when they returned complimented the captain on the cleanliness of the vessel. They staid a short time talking to us upon deck, and the account they gave of the horrid condition of many of the ships in quarantine was frightful. In the holds of some of them they said, that they were up to their ancles in filth. The wretched emigrants crowded together like cattle, and corpses remaining long unburied, the sailors being ill, and the passengers unwilling to touch them. They also told us of the vast numbers of sick in the hospitals, and in tents, upon the island, and that many nuns, clergymen and doctors, were lying in typhus fever, taken from the patients. They were exceedingly intelligent and gentlemanly men, and telling us that we had great cause of thankfulness in having escaped much better than so many others, they politely bowed, and got into their little boat, amid the blessings of the passengers, who watched them until they arrived beside a distant ship.

The Head committee expressed himself satisfied that his wife saw a priest before her death, which occurred about an hour after; and as the pilot said that the remains should not be thrown into the river, there being a burial ground upon the island, the corpse lay in the hold until the next day.

The mate continued to grow worse, and the mistress was unceasing in her attention to him. The day was exceedingly hot and sultry, and I could not have remained on deck, but the captain spread an awning over it, which kept the cabin cool. We lay at some distance from the island, the distant view of which was exceedingly beautiful. At the far end were rows of white tents and marquees, resembling the encampment of an army; somewhat nearer was the little fort, and residence of the superintendent physician, and nearer still the chapel, seaman's hospital, and little village, with its wharf and a few sail boats; the most adjacent extremity being rugged rocks, among which grew beautiful fir trees. At high water this portion was detached from the main island, and formed a most picturesque islet. But this scene of natural beauty was sadly deformed by the dismal display of human suffering that it presented; — helpless creatures being carried by sailors over the rocks, on their way to the hospital, — boats arriving with patients, some of whom died in their transmission from their ships. Another and still more awful sight, was a continuous line of boats, each carrying its freight of dead to the burial-ground, and forming an endless funeral procession. Some had several corpses, so tied up in canvass that the stiff, sharp outline of death was easily traceable; others had rude coffins, constructed by the sailors, from the boards of their berths, or I should rather say, cribs. In a few, a solitary mourner attended the remains; but the majority contained no living beings save the rowers.

I could not remove my eyes until boat after boat was hid by the projecting point of the island, round which they steered their gloomy way. From one ship, a boat proceeded four times during the day; each time laden with a cargo of dead. I ventured to count the number of boats that passed, but had to give up the sickening task.

The inspecting doctor went about from vessel to vessel, six of which came in each tide, and as many sailed.

We expected him to visit us every moment; but he did not come near us.

In the afternoon a boat made for our brig, and the mistress, who was on deck, was greatly delighted to find that it contained two "captains," one of whom was her nephew. One arrived the day before we came; the other a day previous. They were as ignorant of the course of proceeding as we; and before they went away it was agreed on, that they, our captain, and I, should wait on the superintendent physician the next day.

CHAPTER XI.

As from the wing no scar the sky retains,
The parted wave no furrow from the keel,
So dies in human hearts the thought of death.
E'en with the tears which nature shed
O'er those we love, we drop it in their graves. · YOUNG.

Friday, July 30th.

THIS morning, when I came on deck, a sailor was busily
employed constructing a coffin for the remains of the
Head committee's wife; and it was afflicting to hear
the husband's groans and sobs accompanying each sound
of the saw and hammer, while with his motherless infant
in his arms he looked on. About an hour after, the boat
was lowered, and the bereaved husband, with four rowers,
proceeded to the burial ground to inter the corpse; and
they were followed by many a tearful eye, until the boat
disappeared behind the rocky point.

At 10, A. M., we descried the doctor making for us, his
boatmen pulling lustily through the heavy sea; a few minutes brought him alongside and on board, when he ran
down to the cabin and demanded if the papers were filled
up with a return of the number of deaths at sea? how
many cases of sickness? &c. He was handed them by
the captain; when he enquired, — how many patients we
then had; he was told there were twelve; when he wrote

an order to admit six to hospital: saying that the rest should
be admitted when there was room: there being 2500 at
that time upon the island, and hundreds lying in the various vessels before it. The order written, he returned to
his boat, and then boarded a ship lying close to us, which
lowered her signal when he approached. Several other
vessels that arrived in the morning, had their ensigns flying
at the peak, until each was visited in turn.

Immediately after the doctor left us, the captain gave
orders to have the patients in readiness. Shortly after,
our second boat was launched, and four of the passengers volunteered to row; the sailors that were able to
work, being with the other. O God! may I never again
witness such a scene as that which followed; — the husband, — the only support of an emaciated wife and helpless
family, — torn away forcibly from them, in a strange land;
the mother dragged from her orphan children, that clung to
her until she was lifted over the bulwarks, rending the air
with their shrieks; children snatched from their bereaved
parents, who were perhaps ever to remain ignorant of their
recovery, or death. The screams pierced my brain; and
the excessive agony so rent my heart, that I was obliged to
retire to the cabin, where the mistress sat weeping bitterly.

The captain went in the boat, and returned in about an
hour; giving us a frightful account of what he witnessed
upon the island.

The steamers returned, and all the afternoon were engaged, taking the *healthy* passengers out of some of the
vessels; they went alongside several until their cargo was
complete, when they sailed for Montreal, their decks thickly
crowded with human beings; and most extraordinary to

relate, each of them had a fiddler, and a dancing party in
the prow.

Early in the evening the captain's nephew came to take
us in his boat, on shore. After a long pull through a heavy
swell, we landed upon the Isle of Pestilence; and climbing
over the rocks passed through the little town, and by the
hospitals, behind which were piles upon piles of unsightly
coffins. A little further on, at the edge of a beautiful sandy
beach, were several tents, into one of which I looked, but
had no desire to see the interior of any others. We pursued our way, by a road cut through a romantic grove of
firs, birch, beech, and ash, beneath the shade of which grew
and blossomed charming wild flowers, while the most cu-
rious fungi vegetated upon odd, decayed stumps. The path
led us into a cleared lawn, passing through which, we arrived in front of the superintendent physician's cottage, placed
upon a sloping bank at the river's side, on which were
mounted two pieces of ordnance guarded by a sentinel.
The view from this spot was exquisitely beautiful;—upon
the distant bank of the broad river were the smiling, happy-
looking Canadian villages, backed by deep, blue hills, while
the agitated water in front tossed the noble vessels that lay
at anchor, and which were being swung round by the turning tide.

The doctor not being within, we walked about until his
return; when he invited us into his cottage and heard what
the captains had to say; after which he promised to discharge our friend the next day, and that he would send a
steamer to take our passengers. He also gave the captain
an order for the admission of the mate to the seaman's hospital. Our mission having been so successful, we thanked

the doctor and departed. Upon our return we called at the store licensed to sell provisions upon the island. It was well stocked with various commodities, among which were carrion beef, and cattish mutton, bread, flour, cheese, &c. Although the captain wished to treat the mistress to fresh meat, he declined purchasing what we saw, and merely bought some flour. The storekeeper did not lack better customers, however, for there was a vast concourse of mates, stewards, seamen, and boys, buying his different articles, and stowing them away in their boats. The demand for bread was very great; and several batches were yielded from a large oven, while we remained.

Hearing the music of a fiddle accompanied by the stamping of feet in time with the tune, I walked up to the shed from which it issued. There were two men dancing a jig; one of them a Canadian, the other a sailor, — both fine fellows, who were evidently pitted against each other, in a trial of skill. The former wore huge boots coming above the knees, and drawn over his gray trowsers composed of "etoffe du pays," — a light blue flannel shirt confined at the waist by a scarlet scarf, whose parti colored ends hung at one side. On his head was a woollen "bonnet rouge," whose tassel jumped about with the wearer's movements. His brilliant black eyes lighted up his sallow visage, and his arms were as busily engaged as his legs. The sailor was rigged out in pumps, white trowsers, blue jacket, and straw hat with streaming black ribands; his ruddy face glowing with the exercise. The fiddler's costume was similar to that of his brother Canadian, except that his "bonnet" was blue; he stood upon a barrel; and around the dancers was a circle of "habitans" and sailors, who encouraged them by repeated "bravos." I did not remain long, nor could I enjoy the amusement in such a place; and therefore joined my companions in the boat: where we were detained a few moments, while one of the men returned for lime, which the captain had forgotten to procure. He soon returned, and again ploughing through the waves, we shortly arrived beneath the "Leander;" after examining which noble ship, the captain and I returned to the brig, and acquainted the mistress with the issue of our adventure.

Our boat returned, just at the same time; the men having been away all the day. It appeared that they could not find the burial ground, and consequently dug a grave upon an island, when as they were depositing the remains they were discovered, and obliged to decamp. They were returning to the brig, when they perceived several boats proceeding in another direction, and having joined them, were conducted to the right place. The wretched husband was a very picture of desperation and misery, that increased the ugliness of his countenance;—for he was sadly disfigured by the marks of small pox, and was blind of an eye. He walked moodily along the deck, snatched his child from a woman's arms, and went down into the hold without speaking a word. Shortly after, one of the sailors who was with the boat told me, that after the grave was filled up, he took the shovels and placing them cross-wise upon it, calling heaven to witness said, "By that cross, Mary, I swear to revenge your death; as soon as I earn the price of my passage home, I'll go back, and shoot the man that murdered you, and that's the landlord."

Saturday, July 31st.

It was with great reluctance the mate consented to go to

hospital, and as he went into the boat he charged the captain, the mistress, and me with cruelty. The captain went with him, and gave him in charge of a doctor.

In consequence of the superintendent's promise to send a steamer to take our passengers, and to give us clean bills if the vessel were well whitewashed between decks, the passengers' births were all knocked away, and the filthy boards thrown into the river; after which four men worked away cleaning and whitening all the day; but no steamer arrived that day. One which lay over night, took 250 passengers from the captain's nephew, who sailed not long after. Vessels were arriving with every tide; two ships from Bremen came in the morning and were discharged at once, having no sickness; some others sailed up with the evening tide, after which there were more than thirty in quarantine. Boats were plying all day long, between the several vessels and the island; and the sea being high the miserable patients were drenched by the spray; after which they had to clamber over the slimy rocks, or were carried by sailors. There was also an almost unbroken line of boats carrying the dead for interment; then there was the doctor's boat unceasingly shooting about; besides several others containing captains of ships, many of whom had handsome gigs with six oars, and uniformly-dressed rowers. It was indeed a busy scene of life and death. To complete the picture, the rigging of the vessels was covered over with the passengers' linen, hanging out to dry; by the character of which as they fluttered in the breeze, I could tell with accuracy from what country they came; alas! the wretched rags of the majority told but too plainly that they were Irish.

CHAPTER XII.

O the tender ties,
Close twisted with the fibres of the heart,
Which broken break them, and drain off the soul
Of human joy; and make it pain to live.   YOUNG.

Sunday, August 1st.

THE passengers passed a miserable night, huddled up, as
they were without room to stretch their weary limbs. I
pitied them from my soul, and it was sickening to see
them drink the filthy water. I could not refuse to give one
or two of them a mouthful from the cask upon the quarter
deck, which fortunately was filled lower down the river.
They asked for it so pitifully, and were so thankful; but I
could not satisfy all and regretted the disappointment of
many.

They had on their best clothes, and were all clean, with
the exception of one incorrigible family. The doctor came
on board in the forenoon, to inspect the passengers, who
were all called on deck, but those who were unable. Placing himself at a barrier, he allowed each to pass, one by
one; making those he suspected of being feverish, show
their tongues. This proceeding lasted about a quarter of
an hour; when the doctor went into the hold to examine
those below, and to see if it were clean; he then wrote out
the order to admit the six patients to hospital, and promised
to send the steamer to take the remainder; after which we
should have clean bills. When he had gone, the patients

were lowered into the boat amid a renewal of the indescribable woe that followed the previous separations. Two of them were orphan sisters, who were sent for by a brother in Upper Canada. Another was a mother, who had tended all her family through illness, — now careworn, and heartbroken, she became herself a prey.

In the early part of the voyage, I observed the unfilial conduct of a boy, who frequently abused, and even cursed his mother, following the example set by his wretched father. On one occasion, his hand was raised to strike her, when his arm was arrested by a bystander; but the poor woman begged of the man not to punish him, and wept for the depravity of her son. It was she who was now being carried to the boat; while the boy who cursed and would have stricken her, clung to her, crying, and imploring her blessing and forgiveness; but she was unable to utter a word, and by an effort raised her arm feebly and looked sadly upon the afflicted boy, who seized her hand and bathed it with his tears, until he was torn away, and she dropped into the boat, which a moment after rowed off. I felt much for the poor fellow, who was conscious that he should never again see his mother; for there was no hope of her recovery; and I little thought that any one could be so heartless as to aggravate his sufferings, as did two or three women who surrounded him, one of them saying, "Ha! you villain, there's the mother you abused, and cursed, you rascal! you may now take your last look at her." He followed the boat with his eyes, until it reached the shore; when he beheld the inanimate figure borne to the hospital. It was evident from the poignancy of his sorrow, that his heart was not depraved, but that his mis-

5*

conduct arose from education. The morning was fine,
clear and warm, and many of the vessels were decorated
with their flags, giving a cheerful aspect to the scene,
which alas, was marred by the ensigns of two ships (one
on either side of us), which were hoisted half-mast high,
the captain of one, and the chief mate of the other, being
dead. While the captain was away with the boat the
steamer came alongside of us to take our passengers. It
did not take very long to transship them, as few of them
had any luggage. Many of them were sadly disappointed
when they learned that they were to be carried on to Montreal, as those who had left their relatives upon Grosse Isle,
hoped, that as Quebec was not far distant, they would be
enabled by some means to hear of them, by staying there.
Each of them shook hands with the mistress, and all
heaped blessings upon her head ; and as to the captain,
one of them remarked that "though he was a divil, he was
a gintleman."

The steamer pushed off, amid the cheers of her motley
freight, and was soon out of sight. The mistress was
quite overcome by the expressions of the poor creatures'
gratitude for her unceasing, and otherwise unrequited
attention, and benevolence. The captain returned, and
after dinner he and I went ashore for our clean bills of
health. We saw Dr. Douglass, who informed us that the
inspecting physician, Dr. Jaques, had them, and that he
was going his rounds among the vessels; with the intention of calling at the brig. But as we considered that it
would probably be late before he would reach her, we
pulled for a barque, beside which we descried the well
known boat. Before we were half way, it was gone and

making for a ship some distance off; however, we still followed, and again were disappointed. We determined not to give up the chase, and at length caught the doctor on board a German emigrant vessel. He was inspecting the passengers, of whom there were 500, — all of them (without a single exception,) comfortably and neatly clad, clean, and happy. There was no sickness amongst them, and each comely fair haired girl laughed as she passed the doctor, to join the group of robust young men who had undergone the ordeal.

Although it was pleasing to see so many joyous beings, it made me sad when I thought of the very, very different state of my unfortunate compatriots; and I had become so habituated to misery, disease, and death, that the happiness that now surrounded me was quite discordant with my feelings. The doctor having completed his task, countersigned our clean bills, and handed them to the captain; we therefore thanked him and took our leave. Before returning to the brig, we called to see the mate, who was lying with his clothes on, upon a bed; the next one to which contained a figure writhing in torture, and, as the face was turned towards me, I recognized to my great surprise and dismay, the sailor, who, but the evening but one before, was dancing with the Canadian. When the mate perceived us, he rose from the bed, and taking the captain by one arm, and me by the other, walked us both out of the hospital, to the porch; saying that we had no business there, as there was fever upon all sides of us. The hospital was a large chapel, transformed to its present use, and was exceedingly clean and well ventilated, the large windows were all open, causing a draught of air that was agreeable; the evening being very sultry.

We did not remain long with the mate, who raved considerably in his conversation, though he said he was quite well; so, the captain giving him in charge of the attendant, with pressing injunctions to have every attention paid to him, and saying that he hoped he would be able to join the brig upon his return, we departed. As we got into the boat, we made a signal to the pilot (who was desired to be on the lookout,) to weigh anchor, so as not to lose the tide by any unnecessary delay. As we repassed the German ship, the deck was covered with emigrants, who were singing a charming hymn, in whose beautiful harmony all took part; spreading the music of their five hundred voices upon the calm, still air, that wafted it around. The vessel being discharged, began to move almost imperceptibly, so that we quickly passed her; but she gradually gained speed, and was ahead of us by the time we reached the brig, and as the distance between us increased, the anthem died away, until it became inaudible. It was the finest chorus I ever heard, — performed in a theatre of unrivalled magnificence.

The mistress was delighted when she learned that we were free, and all were glad to leave behind the Isle of Death, though we regretted leaving the mate there. The sailors that had been ill, still continuing very weak, the captain induced two young men to remain, in order to assist in working the vessel. At 7 P. M. the anchor was weighed, the sails unreefed, and we glided slowly along.

CHAPTER XIII.

Sail on, sail on, thou fearless bark,
   Wherever blows the welcome wind;
It cannot lead to scenes more dark,
   More sad, than those we leave behind.   MOORE.

Monday, August 2d.

IT was indeed with gratefulness to the Almighty for having preserved me scathless in the midst of the dread pestilence, that I left Grosse Isle; and a more beautiful panorama I never beheld, than the country through which we passed,—the churches of St. Thomas' and St. Pierre's, surrounded by handsome cottages and beautiful fields; on our right Isle Madame, the largest of the numerous islands that clustered in the centre of the river, embosomed in the mighty stream, beyond which rose Cap Tourment, with the village of St. Joachim at its base. And Mount St. Anne, sheltering its village also; both of these lofty hills being of a deep purple hue. At sunset we had reached the eastern extremity of the Isle of Orleans; and an hour after, dropped anchor before St. Francois,— a sweet village composed of quaint looking cottages, whose walls were as white as snow; with red roofs, bright yellow doors, and green venetian window blinds. Such was the universal style, all of them appearing as if they had been newly painted.

We again set sail, soon after day-break this morning, with a breeze against us, which compelled us to tack about.

I did not regret this, as I had many near views of the southern bank of the river, and of the beautiful shore of Orleans island, with its luxuriant orchards and well cultivated farms, sloping down to the water's edge; and dark forest upon the crest of its elevated interior. This fine island, which is 20 miles in length, and five in width, is divided into five parishes, and has a population of 5000 Canadians. While it is an object of the greatest beauty, it is at the same time of great usefulness, affording shelter to the harbor of Quebec on the east side, and producing large supplies of fruits and vegetables of the finest description. The northern shore consists of low and marshy beaches, that abound with game. It is surprising that there is no regular communication between the island and the city, during the summer season; but in winter it is easy of access, over the frozen river, when the inhabitants convey their produce to market. When Cartier visited it in the year 1535, the island was covered with vines, on which account he called it the Isle of Bacchus. It was on it, also, that Wolfe took up his quarters previous to the attack upon Quebec. At 8 A. M. we passed St. Vallier and St. John's; the latter upon the island, consisting of entirely white cottages, which are chiefly inhabited by the branch pilots, upwards of 250 of whom find lucrative employment in the river navigation during the season, enabling them and their families to live comfortably through the long winter, in which they are unemployed.

At noon, we dropped anchor again, before St. Michel's, where we lay until 6 P. M., when we once more renewed our tacks, passing the sheltered cove called Patrick's hole, in which a fine ship rode, previous to leaving port for sea.

This little natural harbour is very valuable, as it securely shelters vessels that arrive before the winter's ice is sufficiently broken up to allow them to gain the city.

At Anse au Maraud, — which is adjacent, there were launched in the year 1824, two enormous ships — the *Columbus* and the *Baron of Renfrew*, which were built with the intention of being broken up in England, the projectors thinking thereby to save the duty on the timber of which they were constructed: but their object was frustrated by the decision that a voyage should previously be made out of an English port. The *Columbus* traversed the Atlantic, and returned in safety; but was wrecked upon her second voyage. The *Baron*, in whose construction six thousand tons of timber were consumed, was 309 feet long, and of proportionate breadth.

She sailed for London on the 25th of August, 1825, with a cargo (it is said of 10,000 tons) of lumber, her four masts crowded with sails, and followed down the river by a fleet of steamers and pleasure yachts. After a voyage of fifty days, she arrived at Dover, where she took on board both Deal and river pilots; but her draft of water being thirty feet, she could not be taken through the queen's channel, which is safe for ships of war. She was therefore obliged to remain outside of the Goodwin sands, near the entrance of the king's channel. Having encountered a violent gale, she grounded upon the Long sands, but was got off on the following day. She safely rode out a second gale upon the 19th of October, but successive storms, and strong northerly winds, eventually drove her upon the Flemish banks, and after being buffeted for several weeks by the waves, she was shattered to atoms; the fragments of the wreck and her cargo being wafted along the coast from Calais to Ostend.

Such was the history of these monster ships, whose ill fortune deterred Canadian builders from again constructing such unwieldly vessels.

We next passed Beaumont, where the south bank becomes elevated, increasing in height to Point Levi, the tin spire of whose church was visible; and on Orleans Island, St. Famille.

The magnificent fall of Montmorenci then was revealed to view, in a sheet of tumbling snow-white foam, set between the dark green banks, covered with fir and other trees. As we approached nearer, the low thundering sound of the "many waters" broke on the ear, which died away as we sailed upon the other tack; and night spread its curtain over the splendid picture, when we reached the mouth of the river St. Charles, where we dropped anchor.

Tuesday, 3d August.

I was charmed with the splendid prospect I enjoyed this morning when I came on deck.

The harbour was thickly covered with vessels, many of them noble ships of the largest class.

The city upon the side of Cape Diamond, with its tin covered dome and spires sparkling in the morning sun, and surrounded by its walls and batteries bristling with cannon, was crowned by the impregnable citadel, while a line of villages spread along the northern shore, reaching to Beauport and Montmorenci. The lofty Mount St. Anne bounding the view upon the east. Opposite the city lay Point Levi, with the village of D'Aubigné; crossing the river were steam ferry-boats, horse-boats, and canoes; and up the stream, — far as the eye could reach, the banks were lined by wharves, and timber ponds, while the breeze wafted along a fleet of batteaux, with great white sails; and numberless pilot boats were in constant motion.

We could not go ashore, neither dare any one come on board, until we were discharged from quarantine by the Harbour Master, and Medical Inspector. These functionaries approached us in a long six-oared boat, with the Union Jack flying in her stern. When they came on board, they demanded the ship's papers, and clean bills of health, which the captain gave them; in return for which he received a release from quarantine. Soon after they left us, a butcher brought us fresh meat, milk, eggs and vegetables, to which we did ample justice at breakfast; when I went with the captain on shore.

I remained with the brig during her stay in Quebec harbour, and sailed in her for Montreal, on the evening of Thursday, 5th August. We were towed up the river by a steamboat; and by daylight the following morning were passing the mouth of the river Batiscan.

The sail during the day was extremely pleasing; true, the St. Lawrence did not present the same grand features as below Quebec, but there was something of exceeding interest or beauty to be seen every moment. The banks varied in height, but did not gain any great elevation, and were lined by an almost unbroken chain of settlements, with villages upon either side at intervals of about ten miles. At noon we sailed by Trois Rivieres, upon the river St. Maurice, which divides into three branches before it empties itself into the St. Lawrence, forming two pretty

islands, connected with each other and the main land by
three handsome bridges.   A couple of hours brought us
into Lake St. Peter, which is an extension of the river, and
of intricate navigation, affording but a narrow channel,
which is marked out by buoys and beacons; towards its
western extremity it is full of low marshy islands, surrounded by rushes, between which lies the winding passage.   At sunset we had a charming view of Sorel, upon
the eastern bank of the Richelieu, which discharges the
waters of lakes George and Champlain.

The river again narrowed, and presented similar features
as below the expansion.   We anchored for the night, and
early next morning were forcing our way through the rapids called current St. Mary, passing the village of Longueil,
and the charming isle St. Helens.   Montreal then opened
to our view, and by 8 A. M. we were moored to its fine
quay.   The brig having completed her cargo, sailed for
London, on the 19th of August, when I bade the captain
and the mistress adieu, and followed them some distance
down the river; until the favorable breeze that filled her
sails, wafted the brig out of sight.   I have represented these
worthy people just as they appeared to me, and if I have
spoken too plainly, I would crave their pardon, should
they ever recognize their lineaments in these sheets, (which
I do not think probable).   Indeed, I should much regret
causing their displeasure, having received from them every
attention; their conduct towards me extending even to un-
wonted kindness, and for which I shall never cease to feel
grateful.   I was anxious to learn if the mate recovered, and
in compliance with my desire the captain wrote to me
from Quebec, and also from Green Island.   The first of

these letters was dated August 23d, and the following is an extract from it :

"I got doun hear on satterday and saled all the way down which was a great saving to me it was bubful sale we Ankered all night and saled in the day which gave hus opertunety of seeing every Curisity we went on Shore and got Eags and milk and sead a little of the Contry this Mornning I am gowing on Shore if there be any Letters for you I will foward them to you I have not heard of my Mate Ariving hear yet which Disapoints me Greatly I wish you had bean with hus Yesterday we had a Drive in the Countrey 9 Miles which was a plesent drive and toke tea in the Countrey a long with Cpt ———. I will sale on Tusday Morning My Wife Joyns me in Cinde Regards to you." In justice I must also quote the postscript. "you must Excuse this as I am in a hury." .

The second letter was written on August 27th. In it the captain says, "I am sorey to inform you of my Mate being so hill I coled at Gruss Ile for him and went on shore and it would have hurt you much to have sean him he was mostly but a Skellitan, but though as hill as he was, I should have brought him on Boord if the Docter would Aload me, I have not any hopes of him, he got nerely well, and mite have come up to the ship but as I told you made two frea with is self putting Bottel to is head Docter to my Wife and me we are all well at present which I hope you cape your Helth, my Wife Joyns me in Cind regards to you."

I learned with satisfaction that the brig arrived at her destination in safety, but of the mate's fate I still remain ignorant.

Of the passengers I never afterwards saw but two, both of them young men, who got employment upon the Lachine canal.   The rest wandered over the country, carrying nothing with them but disease ; and that but few of them survived the severity of the succeeding winter, (ruined as their constitutions were,) I am quite confident.

CHAPTER XIV.

Of comfort no man speak.
Let's talk of graves, of worms, and epitaphs;
Make dust our paper, and with rainy eyes
Write sorrow on the bosom of the earth.
Let's choose executors, and talk of wills;
And yet not so — for what can we bequeath,
Save our deposed bodies to the ground?   SHAKSPEARE.

THAT the system of quarantine pursued at Grosse Isle
afforded but a very slight protection to the people of Canada, is too evident from the awful amount of sickness, and
the vast number of deaths that occurred amongst them
during the navigable season of 1847. From the plan
that was adopted, of sending the majority of the emigrants
from the island directly up to Montreal, Quebec did not
suffer so much as that city. However, during the three days
I was there, in the month of August, too many signs of
death were visible; and upon a second and more pro-
longed visit, later in the season, it presented an aspect of ·
universal gloom: the churches being hung in mourning,
the citizens clothed in weeds; and the newspapers record-
ing daily deaths by fever contracted from the emigrants.
To their honor and praise be it spoken, these alarming
consequences did not deter either clergymen or physicians
from the most unremitting zeal in performing their duty,
and it is to be lamented that so many valuable lives were
sacrificed. A paper of the month of September contained
the following paragraph :— " Quarantine Station — Grosse

Isle. The Rev. J. Butler, missionary at Kingsey, went down on tuesday morning, to take his turn in attendance upon the sick at the quarantine station.

" The Rev. Richard Anderson and Rev. N. Gueront came up on the evening of the same day. The former felt indisposed, and thought it prudent to remain in town for the benefit of medical advice. If he should have an attack of fever, the precaution thus early taken will, it is hoped, prevent its proving severe. We regret to say that the Rev. C. J. Morris, recently returned from the station, is now seriously ill with Typhus Fever." The death of the last gentleman is recorded as follows: " Died, this morning at the private hospital at Beauport, of typhus fever, the Rev. Charles J. Morris, A. M., missionary of the church of England, at Portneuf in this district. Mr. Morris contracted the disease which has thus proved fatal to him, in his ministrations to the sick at Grosse Isle. The funeral will take place in the Cathedral church, to-morrow afternoon, at 3 o'clock."

The Rev. Mr. Anderson also died, within a few days of the same period; and that the mortality continued to a late part of the season, appears by the following, from the Boston Journal of December 1st. " We learn from Quebec that Drs. Painchaud and Jackson, and seven or eight Nuns of the Hotel Dieu were sick with the ship fever. One of the Quebec physicians says that mortality among the physicians during the past season has been greater than it was during the Cholera." On Sunday, October 10th, I had the pleasure of listening to a discourse delivered in St. Patrick's chapel by Rev. Mr. McMahon, before he commenced which, he read a list of the names of several persons, (emigrants) who were separated from their families, and who took this method of endeavoring to find them out; the Rev. Gentleman also acknowledged having received several sums of money remitted from parties in Ireland to friends in Canada, amongst which he said were some without signatures, and one of these was directed "To my Aunt Biddy," upon which his Reverence remarked that people should be more particular where money was concerned.

Although (as I have already stated) the great body of emigrants were sent out to Montreal by steamers, all of them could not be so transferred, and many were detained in Quebec, where the Marine and Emigrant Hospital contained during the season, several hundreds, the number that remained upon October 2nd, being 443, of whom 93 were admitted during the week previous, and in which time there were discharged 132, and 46 died.

One of the first objects that appeared to my view upon my arrival in Montreal, was the Emigrant Hospital, upon Point St. Charles, a low tract of ground cut off from the city by the Lachine canal, and on which the Indians were in the habit of encamping every summer before it was turned to its present purpose. On the day I arrived, August 7th, it contained 907 patients, 16 having died during the last 24 hours. An official return of burials in the city was furnished up to the same day, by which it appeared, that during the previous nine weeks the number was 1730, of which 924 were residents, and 806 were emi-. grants. Exclusive of these there died in the sheds, 1510 emigrants, making a total of 3,240, being 2,752 more than occurred during the corresponding period of the preceding year. Upon August 23rd the emigrant sheds contained 1330, 27 having died during twenty-four hours ; and so late as October 11th, there remained 746 patients in them.

Montreal lost many of her most valuable citizens in consequence of the contagion, among whom were Dr. Cushing, and the mayor. Neither was the pestilence stayed here, for the inhabitants of Kingston, Bytown, Toronto, and other places were infected, and a great number died of the fever, amongst whom was the Rev. Dr. Power, R. C. Bishop of Toronto, who contracted the disease in the discharge of his sacred functions among the sick. The following extract, taken from the Toronto Standard, serves to show the manner in which the people of Canada suffered, and their sympathy for those who brought so much woe amongst them. " The health of the city remains in much the same state as it did several weeks ago. The individual cases of fever have abated nothing of their violence, and several families have caught the infection from having admitted emigrants into their houses. The greatest caution should be observed in this respect, as it does not require contact alone, to infect a healthy person with the deadly virus of the fever. Breathing the same atmosphere with the infected, or coming under the influence of the effluvia rising from their clothes is, in some states of the healthy body, perfectly sufficient for effecting a lodgment of the disease in the human frame. On Monday evening last, the report of the Finance Committee, on the subject of erecting a House of Refuge for the destitute persons who have sought refuge in our City, was received by the Council. This committee report in favor of erecting immediately such a building as would shield those gers from the severities of winter, and recommend that a sum not exceeding £5,000 should be expended for that purpose, and that the sum should be put under the joint superintendence of the Board of Works and the Finance Committee, so that now we have from the praiseworthy benevolence and amenity of the Council, an assured hope, that the emigrants will not be exposed to any hardships which it is in the power of the city authorities to ward off."

The reader will bear in mind that the above relates to the city of Toronto, in Western Canada, at a distance of upwards of 500 miles from the Quarantine station, whose stringent regulations were intended to protect the country from contagion.

It now only remains for me to say a few words respecting the people that endured and reproduced so much tribulation.

The vast number of persons who quitted Europe, to seek new homes in the western hemisphere, in the year 1847, is without a precedent in history. Of the aggregate I cannot definitely speak, but to be within the limits of truth, they exceeded 350,000.

More than one half of these emigrants were from Ireland, and to this portion was confined the devouring pestilence. It is a painful task to trace the causes that led to such fatal consequences; some of them may, perhaps, be hidden, but many are too plainly visible. These wretched people were flying from known misery, into unknown and tenfold aggravated misfortune. That famine which compelled so many to emigrate, became itself a cause of the pestilence. But that the principal causes were produced by injustice and neglect, is plainly proved. Many, as I have already

6

stated, were sent out at the expense of their landlords; these were consequently the poorest and most abject of the whole, and suffered the most. No doubt the motives of some landlords were benevolent; but all they did was to pay for the emigrants' passage—this done, these gentlemen washed their hands of all accountability, transferring them to the shipping agent, whose object was to stow away the greatest possible number between the decks of the vessels chartered for the purpose. That unwarrantable induce- ments were held out to many, I am aware, causing some to leave their homes, who would not otherwise have done so. They were given to understand that they would be abundantly provided for during the voyage, and that they were certain of finding immediate employment upon their arrival, at a dollar per day. Another serious injury was done many families, who had previously experienced the blessings of temperance, from being, upon their arrival at the different ports where they were to embark, obliged to lodge in public houses of the worst description; whose proprietors, knowing that they possessed a little stock of money, seduced them to violate their "pledge," under the specious pretext that they were no longer bound by its obligations, and that whiskey was the very best preventive of sea-sickness. After a detention—often of many days, the vessel at length ready for sea, numbers were shipped that were quite unfit for a long voyage. True, they were inspected, and so were the ships, but from the limited number of officers appointed for the purpose, many over- sights occurred. In Liverpool, for instance, if I am rightly informed, there was a staff of but five or six men to inspect the mass of emigrants, and survey the ships, in which there sailed from that port 107,474. An additional heavy

infliction was their sufferings on ship-board, from famine,
the legal allowance for an adult being one pound of food
in twenty-four hours; but perhaps the most cruel wrong
was in allowing crowds of already infected beings to be
huddled up together in the confined holds, there to propa-
gate the distemper, which there was no physician to stay.
The sufferings consequent upon such treatment, I have
endeavoured to portray in the previous narrative, which
alas! is but a feeble picture of the unmitigated trials endured by these most unhappy beings. Nor were their sufferings ended with the voyage. Oh! no, far from it.
Would that I could represent the afflictions I witnessed at
Grosse Isle! I would not be supposed to think, that the
medical officers situated there did not exercise the greatest
humanity in administering their disagreeable duties, which
consisted—not in relieving the distress of the emigrants;
but in protecting their country from contamination. Still
it was most afflicting, that after combatting the dangers of
the sea, enduring famine, drought, and sickness, the wretched survivors should still have to lie as uncared for as when
in the centre of the Atlantic Ocean.

The inefficacy of the quarantine system is so apparent,
that it is needless to particularize its defects, neither need I
repeat the details of the grievous aggravations of their
trials, heaped by it upon the already tortured emigrants.
My heart bleeds when I think of the agony of the poor
families who as yet undivided had patiently borne their
trials, ministering to each other's wants — when torn from
each other. Painful as it was to behold the bodies of those
who died at sea, committed to the deep, yet the separation of families was fraught with much greater misery.
And as if to reach the climax of endurance, the relatives

and friends of those landed upon the island were at once
carried away from them to a distance of 200 miles. On
their way to Montreal, many died on board the steamers.
There, those who sickened in their progress were received
into the hospital, and the survivors of this second sifting
were sent on to Kingston, — 180 miles further; from thence
to Toronto, and so on, — every city and town being anxious
to be rid of them. Nor were there wanting villains, who
preyed upon these stricken people. — The Montreal Herald of October 13th thus writes. " The rapid closing of
the season of course diminishes the number of arrivals of
emigrants, and thus the hospitals and asylums are less
crowded than they have been at an earlier period of the
year. The statements are, however, still extremely dis-
tressing. An assertion has been made in the Common
. Council, and is generally believed to be true, that considerable sums have been brought here by some of these people,
and consigned by them, in their last moments, to persons
who have in many instances appropriated the money to
their own use. An Alderman named Tully, who is known
to have the means of information, calculates the average
of the sums brought to Canada by emigrants at £10
each — we suppose heads of families."

In a tour which I made through Upper Canada, I met
in every quarter some of my poor wandering fellow-coun-
try people. Travelling from Prescott to Bytown, by stage,
I saw a poor woman with an infant in her arms, and a
child pulling at her skirt, and crying as they went along.
The driver compassionately took them up, and the way-
farer wept her thanks. She had lost her husband upon
the voyage, and was going to Bytown to her brother, who
came out the previous year, and having made some money

by lumbering in the woods, remitted to her the means of joining him; she told her sad tale most plaintively, and the passengers all sympathized with her. The road being of that description called "corduroy," and the machine very crazy, the latter broke down within five miles of our destination, and as she was unable to carry her two children, the poor creature was obliged to remain upon the road all the night. She came into Bytown the following morning, and I had the satisfaction to learn that she found her brother.

A large proportion of the emigrants who arrived in Canada crossed the frontiers, in order to settle in the United States. So that they were to be seen in the most remote places. At St. Catherine's, upon the Welland canal, 600 miles from Quebec, I saw a family, who were on their way to the western part of the state of New York. One of them was taken ill, and they were obliged to remain by the wayside; with nothing but a few boards to protect them from the weather. There is no means of learning how many of the survivors of so many ordeals were cut off by the inclemency of a Canadian winter, so that the grand total of the human sacrifice will never be known but by " Him who knoweth all things."

As I cannot so well convey my sentiments in my own language, I will conclude with the following quotation from England's most popular writer, and would that his suggestions uttered five years before the commencement of the tragic drama, had been attended to in time: if they had, much evil had been spared humanity. " The whole system of shipping and conveying these unfortunate persons is one that stands in need of thorough revision. If any class deserve to be protected and assisted by the government, it is that class who are banished from their native land in search of the bare means of subsistence.   All that could be done for those poor people by the great compassion and humanity of the captain and officers, was done, but they require much more.   The law is bound, at least upon the English side, to see that too many of them are not put on board one ship ; and that their accommodations are decent, not demoralizing and profligate.   It is bound, too, in common humanity, to declare that no man shall be taken on board without his stock of provisions being previously inspected by some proper officer, and pronounced moderately sufficient for his support upon the voyage.   It is bound to provide, or to require that there be provided a medical attendant ; whereas in these ships there are none, though sickness of adults and deaths of children on the passage are matters of the very commonest occurrence.   Above all, it is the duty of any government, be it monarchy or republic, to interpose and put an end to that system by which a firm of traders in emigrants purchase of the owners the whole 'tween-decks of a ship, and send on board as many wretched people as they can get hold of on any terms they can get, without the smallest reference to the conveniences of the steerage, the number of berths, the slightest separation of the sexes, or any thing but their own immediate profit.   Nor is this the worst of the vicious system ; for certain crimping agents of these houses, who have a per centage on all the passengers they inveigle, are constantly travelling about those districts where poverty and discontent are rife, and tempting the credulous into more misery, by holding out monstrous inducements to emigration which never can be realized."*

* Dickens. *American Notes.*

APPENDIX.

Immediately a place
Before his eyes appear'd, sad, noisome, dark;
A lazar-house it seem'd; wherein were laid
Numbers of all diseased; all maladies
Of ghastly spasm, or racking torture, qualms
Of heart-sick agony, all feverous kinds,
Marasmus, and wide-wasting pestilence,
Dropsies, and asthmas, and joint-racking rheums,
Dire was the tossing, deep the groans: Despair
Tended the sick, busiest from couch to couch;
And over them triumphant Death his dart
Shook, but delay'd to strike, though oft invoked
With vows, as their chief good, and final hope.
Sight so deform what heart of rock could long
Dry eyed behold?   MILTON.

THE intention of this appendix is, by the means of a few extracts from newspapers, hospital returns, reports, &c., to furnish some further general information respecting the ship pestilence.

But as the previous narrative is not designed to present a history of that sad subject, so neither will this sequel supply complete statistics regarding it. The extracts go no further back than the beginning of August; but will be found sufficient to elucidate the events from that time until the termination of the season.

" Grosse Isle. — Il y avait samedi dernier à la Grosse Isle 2148 malades; du 1er au 6 août 130 personnes sont mortes." — *La Reveu Canadienne.*

" Monday Afternoon, August 9.

" Since my last, the wind has been blowing fresh from

the northeast, and several vessels have arrived in port, the
names of which you will find enclosed. Four have just
arrived, but are not yet boarded. I make out the names
of three, viz:—Bark Covenanter, Bark Royal Adelaide,
and Schooner Maria, of Limerick. The Zealous has not
yet made her appearance.

"The accounts from Grosse Isle since my last, are not
of a favorable nature, and the number of deaths is much
the same. The building of the new sheds there is advanc-
ing rapidly.

"A letter was received this forenoon, from the mate of
the bark Naparima, with passengers, from Dublin, dated
off Bic, last Friday, announcing that the Captain, Thomas
Brierly, died on the 3d instant, and was buried on the same
day. She was then fifty days out, and short of provisions,
—about 20 of the passengers were sick, but were recover-
ing when the mate wrote, and he intended to put into
some convenient place for supplies. There was a pilot
on board, and every exertion would be made to get her up
to the Quarantine Station as soon as possible."

. — *Quebec Correspondence of the Montreal Herald.*

"We are in possession of the latest news from Grosse
Isle. The hospital statement yesterday, the 9th, was 2240.
There is a large fleet of vessels at the station, and amongst
them some very sickly, as it may be seen from the following statement:—

		Passengers.	Deaths.	Sick.
Bark Ellen Simpson,	Limerick,	184	4	—
Brig Anna Maria,	"	119	1	1
Bark Amy,	Bremen,	289	—	—

Brig Watchful,	Hamburg,	145	—	—
Ship Ganges,	Liverpool,	393	45	80
Bark Corea,	"	501	18	7
Bark Larch,	Sligo,	440	108	150
Bark Naparima,	Dublin,	226	7	17
Bark Britannia,	Greenock,	386	4	25
Brig Trinity,	Limerick,	86	all well.	—
Bark Lilias,	Dublin,	219	5	6
Bark Brothers,	"	318	6	—

" A full rigged ship just coming in — not yet boarded.

" The hospitals have never been so crowded, and the poor creatures in the tents (where the healthy are), are dying by dozens! Eleven died on the night of the 8th, and one on the road to the hospital yesterday morning.

" Captain Read, of the Marchioness of Breadalbane, died in hospital on the 7th. The Captain of the Virginius died the day after his arrival at Grosse Isle.

" We regret to learn that the Rev. Mr. Paisley is in a critical state. He was dangerously ill this morning.

" Since writing the above we learn that 60 new cases were admitted into hospital, and 300 more, arrived on the 8th and 9th, remain to be admitted!"

— *Quebec Mercury, August* 10th, 1847.

" The Steamer St. George arrived from Grosse Isle yesterday afternoon, but brought nothing of importance. The cool temperature of the last few days has had a favorable effect on the sick in the tents, and fewer cases of fever had appeared.

6*

"The Ship Washington from Liverpool, 9th of July,
had arrived at the station yesterday. She has one cabin,
and 305 steerage passengers, had 22 deaths and 20 sick.
She reports 15 vessels with passengers in the Traverse.
                                    — *Quebec Chronicle.*

"*Hospital return* — *Grosse Isle, September 14th,* 1847.
          Remaining on 14th,   1386,
          Died 12th to 13th inst.,   41."

"*Hospital return* — *Grosse Isle, from 19th to 25th of Sept.*

Remaining on 19th,	1196,	Discharged,	234,
Admitted since,	436,	Died,	121,
	1632		355
	355		
	1277		

"Deaths at the sheds, where the healthy passengers are
landed, during the same period — 10.

"There are 1240 cases of fever, and 37 cases of small
pox. Two men died whilst being landed from the Emigrant, and 162 cases were admitted into hospital from the
same vessel."

"*Hospital statement to the 28th :*

Men,	473
Women,	441
Children,	349
Total,	1263

Grosse Isle. — *Return of sick in hospitals 1st October.*

		Discharged.	Died.	Remaining.
Men,	414	103	7	304
Women,	412	156	3	253
Children,	326	109	1	216
	1152	368	11	773

(Signed) I. M. Douglass, *Med. Sup.*

" About 400 convalescents went up to Montreal in the Canada on Thursday last, and 35 came up to Quebec in the Lady Colborne on Friday.

" This has enabled the Medical Superintendent to close another hospital; and this day the services of two more medical men, with their staff of orderlies and nurses will be dispensed with."

" *Hospital statement, 5th October.*

" Men, 230 — Women, 124 — Children, 150 — Total, 504·

" There were then three vessels with emigrants at the station."

" A MELANCHOLY TALE OF WOE.

" On Saturday last, 30th October, the Lord Ashburton, from Liverpool, 13th September, with general cargo and passengers, arrived at Grosse Isle in a most wretched state.

" When sailing she had 475 steerage passengers, and before her arrival at the Quarantine Station, she had lost 107 by dysentery and fever; and about 60 of those remaining were then ill of the same complaints. So deplorable was the condition of those on board that five of the passengers had to remain to work the ship up from Grosse Isle." — *Quebec Mercury.*

" EMIGRATION FROM LIVERPOOL.

" The amount of emigration from Great Britain and Ireland has this year far surpassed that of any previous year, as will be seen from the following returns, made up on the 6th instant, of emigration from this port alone: —

United States,	77,403
Canada,	27,666
New Brunswick,	1,479
Nova Scotia,	171
Prince Edward's Isle,	444
Other places,	311
Total,	107,474

" Of this vast number of emigrants, two thirds were Irish, and of the remaining one third, two fifths were Scotch and English, and one fifth German, of whom a larger number than formerly left this port during the past season."

Reports of the following vessels upon their arrival at Grosse Isle ; namely,

		Passengers.	Deaths.	Sick.
Sir Henry Pottinger,	Cork,	399	98	112
Bark Wellington,	Liverpool,	435	26	30
Bark Sir Robert Peel,	"	458	24	12
Schooner Jessie,	Limerick,	108	2	16
Bark Anne Rankin,	Glasgow,	332	7	3
Bark Zealous,	London,	120	1	5

" We are glad to learn that the *Sœurs Grises*,* amongst

---

* The Gray Sisters, a community of charitable Nuns.

whom sickness and death have made such fearful havoc, during their self-immolating ministrations to the dying emigrants, are again pursuing their charitable labors at the Sheds at Point St. Charles. We are happy to learn, also, that the sickness in Griffintown is rapidly on the decrease." — *Montreal Pilot.*

The following advertisement is a specimen of many of a similar nature, that daily appeared in the newspapers; and requires no comment.

" Information wanted of Abraham Taylor, aged 12 years, Samuel Taylor, 10 years, and George Taylor, 8 years old, from county Leitrim, Ireland, who landed in Quebec about five weeks ago — their mother having been detained at Grosse Isle. Any information respecting them will be thankfully received by their brother, William Taylor, at this office." — *Montreal Transcript,* September 11th, 1847.

" The ' Quebec Chronicle' having obtained permission to copy them from the official records, has commenced the publication of the names of all the unfortunates who have died in the hospital at Grosse Isle, with their ages and the names of the vessels in which they came to Canada, as well as the date of the decease. The ' Chronicle' deserves well of the community, for thus affording the relatives of the poor sufferers the means of knowing what has become of them." — *Montreal Courier.*

" The immigration commissioners report that 94 vessels have landed in the Province of New Brunswick, the present season, 15,269 passengers. The deaths at sea on board these vessels, were six hundred and sixty two."

" The schooner Victoria, from Quebec, with 20 passengers, anchored at the Quarantine ground on Tuesday last.
She had three cases of typhus fever on board. The passengers and crew were landed on Middle Island this morning, the captain securing the maintainance of the healthy
passengers and crew until discharged." — *Miramichi
Gleaner*, 27th July.

" *Emigration to New York.* — We have received from
Senator Folsom a printed copy of the report forwarded to
the Legislature by the Commissioners of Emigration at
this port. It is dated October 1st, 1847. The board of
Commissioners having been organized on the 8th May
last, Robert Taylor being appointed agent, and William
F. Havemeyer, president — proceeded immediately to take
charge of the sick and destitute emigrants. Having filled
the Quarantine hospitals, all the spare rooms connected
with the City Almshouse department were hired at a dollar per week for each destitute emigrant, and a dollar and
a half per week for the sick. But the introduction of fever
patients at the Almshouse was·attended with too much
risk, and buildings were erected for their accommodation on
Staten Island. These being still inadequate, the buildings
on the Long Island Farms were leased, but the fear of
contagion so alarmed the neighborhood, that the buildings
were burned by incendiaries.

The United States Government at once granted their
warehouses at Quarantine for the accommodation of the
sick. They were soon filled, as all the principal hospitals,
public and private, to which the Commissioners had to
resort. At this crisis, a large stone building was leased on

Ward's Island, which with buildings subsequently added to it, afforded ample accommodation for the thousands dependent upon their benevolent undertaking.

"Many were destitute of clothing, and from May to September, ten thousand three hundred and eight articles of dress were made at Ward's Island and furnished to them, by direction of the Commissioners. Hundreds have been provided with employment in the interior of the state, and many forwarded West at the expense of the Commissioners.

"The number of passengers who arrived from May 5th to Sept. 30th, inclusive, and for whom commutation money was paid, or bonds given, was 101,546, of whom only 25 were bonded.

"Of said passengers there were natives of

Germany,	43,208	Italy,	130
Ireland,	40,820	Sweden,	119
England and Wales,	6,501	Spain,	72
Holland,	2,966	Denmark,	51
France,	2,633	Portugal,	31
Scotland,	1,856	Poland,	21
Switzerland,	1,506	East Indies,	6
Norway,	881	Turkey,	1
Belgium,	478	South America,	1
West Indies,	265		
		Total,	101,546

Of which number there were

Forwarded from the city.	Temporarily relieved.	Sent to Hospitals.	Sent to Alms house.
427.	217.	5,148.	713.

Total, 6,505, of whom were Irish 3,792.

"Adding to the above 256 emigrants who were in Hospital at the time the Commissioners entered upon their duties, we have 6,761, the total number under their care up to the date of this report.

"Of these, seven hundred and three died between the 8th of May and the 1st October. The names, ages, and places of birth, of the dead, are not given. This is an oversight which ought to be corrected.

"It seems, also, that no provision was made for the erection of any memorial over their graves." — *New York Paper.*

"*Ship Fever.* — The British ship India, Gray, (late Thompson), arrived yesterday from Liverpool, after a passage of 57 days. Captain Thompson died of the ship fever on the 14th inst., (January, 1848) and during the passage 39 of the passengers died of the same disease. The chief officer of the ship, and a large number of the passengers are now sick. When the India left Liverpool she had two hundred and seventy passengers."

— *New York Express.*

"The British Ship Viceroy, arrived at New Orleans on the 5th instant, with 286 immigrants.

"Fourteen had died on the passage, and many others were very sick, and sent to the Charity Hospital. The Orizaba, which arrived from Liverpool on the 31st ult., had shipped 170 ; 24 of whom died, and most of the rest were sent to the Hospital." — *Boston Mail, Jan.* 19th, 1848.

" Report of Deer Island Hospital, Boston, for the week ending January 8th, 1848.

Number remaining as per last week's report,	311	
Admitted since,	28	
Total	—	339
Discharged,	36	
Died,	13	49
Remaining,		290
Whole number admitted to this date,		2,330
Whole number buried on the Island,		347
Of whom were brought from the ship dead,		20
Died the day of their reception,		8
In carriage,		2 "

— *Boston Journal.*

" FOREIGN EMIGRANTS. — A communication from the State Department was laid before the House of Representatives on Friday last, reporting the number of passengers who arrived from foreign countries on shipboard, during the year ending the 30th of September last. The number of males was 139,166; females, 99,325; sex not reported, 989; total, 239,480. The prospect is that the number will be much larger the present year.

" Of the above number of passengers, 145,838 landed in New York; 20,848 in Massachusetts; 5,806 in Maine; 14,777 in Pennsylvania; 12,018 in Maryland; 34,803 in Louisiana, and 3,873 in Texas." — *Boston Journal.*

Abstract statement of payments on account of the expenses attending emigration, in the Province of Canada, during the season 1847. Taken from the Inspector General's report.

Amount paid for the erection of Hospital Sheds.

At Grosse Isle,	£10,609,	11,	7
At Quebec,	1,120,	0,	0
At Montreal,	15,914,	17,	5
	£27,644,	9,	0
For transport of emigrants inland, including cost of provisions,	35,450,	0,	0
For Boards of Health.			
Canada, East and West,	60,220,	19,	7
Expenses at Quarantine Station,	15,465,	17,	6
Emigration Agent for transport,	10,502,	4,	5
Board of Health, and Emigrant Hospital at Quebec,	8,000,	0,	0
Total,	£157,283	10,	6

Table showing the comparative number of emigrants to the ports designated, viz:

	1846	1847	Increase 1847
Quebec,	32,753	98,105	65,352
New York,	97,843	145,890	48,047
New Orleans,	22,148	40,442	18,294
Boston,	14,079	20,745	6,666
Philadelphia,	7,236	14,763	7,527
Baltimore,	9,327	12,018	2,691
	183,386	331,963	148,577

" EMIGRATION TO BRITISH NORTH AMERICA.

" Emigration returns just issued by order of her Majesty, state that the numbers who embarked in Europe, in 1847, for Canada, was 98,006.   Viz:

* From England,	32,228	
From Ireland,	54,329	
From Scotland,	3,752	
, From Germany,	7,697	
	———	
		98,006

Of the whole number 91,882 were steerage passengers, 684 cabin, and 5541 infants. Deducting from this aggregate the Germans and the cabin passengers, the entire number of emigrants who embarked at British ports was 89,738, of whom 5,293 died before their arrival, leaving 84,445 who reached the colony. Of these it is estimated that six sevenths were from Ireland. Of the 84,445 who reached the colony alive, no less than 10,037 died after their arrival. Of the remainder no less than 30,265 were admitted into Hospital for medical treatment. Up to the 12th of November last, the number of destitute emigrants forwarded from the agency at Montreal to Upper Canada was 38,781." — *New Orleans Price Current.*

As the conduct of Irish landlords has been severely commented upon, in the foregoing pages, it is but just to inform the reader of a most honorable exception; and which it affords the author extreme gratification to be enabled to do, by transcribing the following article from the "British Canadian."

"LAST SEASON'S EMIGRATION.

" Among the landlords who last summer were desirous of providing an asylum for a portion of their tenantry, was

---

* It may be necessary to remark that many of the Irish emigrants sailed from English ports.

one who was actuated by far other motives than merely
getting rid of so many people.   We trust there were others
urged by similar motives, but there were some not very
creditable exceptions.   Steven E. De Vere, Esq., a gentleman of fortune, and the proprietor of some estates in the
South of Ireland, having heard a great deal about the evils
and benefits of emigration to this Province, and hearing
also of the sufferings of many poor people who had been
sent from the country, determined to try the experiment
himself.   This he came to the conclusion to do, not
by making arrangements for the transport of so many
hundreds of thousands of his tenantry, and remaining at
home to hear as much, or as little as might be, of their
fate; but he would see for himself.   He accordingly picked
some dozen volunteers from among the numbers who
would gladly have accompanied him, and with them took
shipping for Quebec, in the steerage of one of the regular
passenger ships.   Landlord and Tenant fared alike, the
former taking careful notes of the events of the passage.
Of the voyage we need say nothing more than that it was
of the average character — there was all the disease, ill
usage, and wretchedness of which our readers have often
been made perfectly aware ;— the state of things which
imported the fever that carried off many of our most
valued friends and citizens.   At Quebec, proceedings were
commenced against the Captain, which were ultimately
compounded upon his paying a certain amount for the
benefit of the suffering Emigrants.   Mr. De Vere proceeded
to Upper Canada, and closely observed the whole process
of transportation, to the very last destination — the graves
of the fever-stricken people.   In Toronto this philanthropic

gentleman attended the emigrant office, and rendered much assistance to the lamented and indefatigable agent, Mr. Mc Elderly, boarding with him every steamer filled with the wretched cargoes, and transmitting to the "proper authorities" the result of his laborious experience. He was well pleased with the management of our hospitals; but shocked, as every one was, with the mode of transporting the poor people hither. Some of the steamboat cargoes were sufficient to recall to the mind the horrors of the sea voyage. Mr. De Vere's people suffered from fever, but recovered, receiving his constant personal attendance. The fact of this gentleman's investigations being laid before the Colonial Secretary, and some members of the House of Lords, coming as they did from one well known, and who could not possibly have any interest in writing, but the benefit of his countrymen, has had a good effect, and he merits well of the people of this Province, as well as the emigrating population of the mother country.

Few men are found to act from such pure disinterestedness in these days, and it is gratifying to observe the result of such labors.

Mr. De Vere returns shortly to England, and, by making his views public, will, we hope, be the means of obtaining further improvements, as those already made are by no means sufficient. One fact is certain, his information may be implicitly relied upon by government; for he has obtained it himself, on the spot, and by the most careful, and indeed dangerous investigation, as the above mentioned facts fully show."

It was the author's intention to confine himself to the

occurrences of the year 1847; but as the publication of the foregoing narrative has been delayed longer than was anticipated, it may here be observed that he had strong hopes that judicious precautions would have been taken to prevent the repetition this season, of the tragic scenes of the last.

Some legislative enactments for the further regulation of Emigrant ships have been passed by Great Britain, during the last session of Parliament; but it is much to be feared that they will prove quite inefficient. It is painful to observe the very unfavorable accounts from some of the Ports of the United States, as well as of New Brunswick and Nova Scotia.

As regards Canada the prospect is exceedingly gloomy, to judge from the conduct of the executive government *in forbidding the publication, or issue of any reports from the Quarantine Station*, respecting the state of things there.

Were not the trials of the wretched emigrant already sufficiently great, that he must

" To such unsightly sufferings be debased ? "

The Press has boldly taken up the matter, and it is to be hoped that the appearance and repetition of such articles as the following will tend to the repeal of the obnoxious and cruel edict.

" GROSSE ISLE INTELLIGENCE.

" The executive government have forbidden the transmission of any news or statements from the island, except, we suppose, to head quarters, that is, to themselves. This is a proceeding as arrogant as it is absurd and mischievous.

Last year full reports were given to the public of the state of the island and the proceedings there, as well from official as from private sources. Why then interdict the publication this year, when more than ever a faithful return of the health and sickness prevailing at the quarantine station is most desirable?

If the prohibition be intended to prevent alarm, it is founded upon false premises, as, in the absence of authentic information, wild and exaggerated rumors obtain credence. The public have a right to be informed of what is passing at Grosse Isle." — *Kingston Chronicle*, 17th June, 1848.

It is unnecessary to bring forward any further evidence of the popular indignation so warmly expressed against such despotic cruelty. How long will

> " Oppression, with her heart
> Wrapp'd up in triple brass, besiege mankind ? "

THE END.

THE OCEAN PLAGUE:

OR,

A VOYAGE TO QUEBEC IN AN IRISH EMIGRANT VESSEL.

EMBRACING

A QUARANTINE AT GROSSE ISLE IN 1847. WITH NOTES ILLUSTRATIVE OF
THE SHIP-PESTILENCE OF THAT FATAL YEAR.

BY A CABIN PASSENGER.

"To that a starving and diseased peasant under the eyes of Quebec, ought to be punishable as murder."
LORD BROUGHAM.

BOSTON:
COOLIDGE AND WILEY, 12 WATER STREET.
1848.